Acting Edition

MW01075447

Purlie
Victorious

A Comedy in Three Acts

by Ossie Davis

ISBN 978-0-573-61435-4

www.concordtheatricals.com
www.concordtheatricals.co.uk

No one shall make any changes in this title(s) for the purpose of production. No part of this book may be reproduced, stored in a retrieval system, scanned, uploaded, or transmitted in any form, by any means, now known or yet to be invented, including mechanical, electronic, digital, photocopying, recording, videotaping, or otherwise, without the prior written permission of the publisher. No one shall share this title(s), or any part of this title(s), through any social media or file hosting websites.

For all inquiries regarding motion picture, television, online/digital and other media rights, please contact Concord Theatricals Corp.

MUSIC AND THIRD-PARTY MATERIALS USE NOTE

Licensees are solely responsible for obtaining formal written permission from copyright owners to use copyrighted music and/or other copyrighted third-party materials (e.g. artworks, logos) in the performance of this play and are strongly cautioned to do so. If no such permission is obtained by the licensee, then the licensee must use only original music and materials that the licensee owns and controls. Licensees are solely responsible and liable for clearances of all third-party copyrighted materials, including without limitation music, and shall indemnify the copyright owners of the play(s) and their licensing agent, Concord Theatricals Corp., against any costs, expenses, losses and liabilities arising from the use of such copyrighted third-party materials by licensees. For music, please contact the appropriate music licensing authority in your territory for the rights to any incidental music.

IMPORTANT BILLING AND CREDIT REQUIREMENTS

If you have obtained performance rights to this title, please refer to your licensing agreement for important billing and credit requirements.

PURLIE VICTORIOUS premiered on September 28, 1961, at the Cort Theatre, New York City. It was presented by Philip Rose and directed by Howard Da Silva. Settings and lighting were by Ben Edwards, with costumes by Ann Roth. The production stage manager was Leonard Auerbach, and the assistant stage manager was John Sillings. The cast was as follows:

PURLIE VICTORIOUS JUDSON. . . . . Ossie Davis

LUTIEBELLE GUSSIE MAE JENKINS . . . . Ruby Dee

MISSY JUDSON . . . . Helen Martin

GITLOW JUDSON . . . . Godfrey M. Cambridge

CHARLIE COTCHIPEE. . . . . Alan Alda

IDELLA LANDY . . . . Beah Richards

OL' CAP'N COTCHIPEE. . . . . Sorrell Booke

THE SHERIFF . . . . Ci Herzog

THE DEPUTY . . . . Roger C. Carmel

The revival of *PURLIE VICTORIOUS* was produced by Jeffrey Richards, Hunter Arnold, Leslie Odom, Jr., Louise Gund, and Bob Boyett, and opened on September 27, 2023, at the Music Box Theatre, New York City. The performance was directed by Kenny Leon, with scenic design by Derek McLane, costume design by Emilio Sosa, lighting design by Adam Honoré, and sound design by Peter Fitzgerald. The production stage manager was Kamra A. Jacobs. The cast was as follows:

PURLIE VICTORIOUS JUDSON. . . . . Leslie Odom, Jr.

LUTIEBELLE GUSSIE MAE JENKINS . . . . Kara Young

MISSY JUDSON . . . . Heather Alicia Simms

GITLOW JUDSON . . . . Billy Eugene Jones

CHARLIE COTCHIPEE. . . . . Noah Robbins

IDELLA LANDY . . . . Vanessa Bell Calloway

OL' CAP'N COTCHIPEE. . . . . Jay O. Sanders

THE SHERIFF . . . . Bill Timoney

THE DEPUTY . . . . Noah Pyzik

CHARACTERS

(In Order of Appearance)

PURLIE VICTORIOUS JUDSON
LUTIEBELLE GUSSIE MAE JENKINS
MISSY JUDSON
GITLOW JUDSON
CHARLIE COTCHIPEE
IDELLA LANDY
OL' CAP'N COTCHIPEE
THE SHERIFF
THE DEPUTY

SETTING

The cotton plantation country of the Old South

TIME

The recent past

"Our churches will say segregation is immoral because it makes perfectly wonderful people, white and black, do immoral things; ...

Our courts will say segregation is illegal because it makes perfectly wonderful people, white and black, do illegal things; ...

And finally our Theatre will say segregation is ridiculous because it makes perfectly wonderful people, white and black, do ridiculous things!"

– From "Purlie's I.O.U."

ACT I

Scene One

(Scene: The setting is the plain and simple interior of an antiquated, run-down farmhouse such as Negro sharecroppers still live in, in South Georgia. Threadbare but warm-hearted, shabby but clean. In the center is a large, rough-hewn table with three homemade chairs and a small bench. This table is the center of all family activities. The main entrance is a door in the upstage right corner, which leads in from a rickety porch which we cannot see. There is a small archway in the opposite corner, with some long strips of gunny-sacking hanging down to serve as a door, which leads off to the kitchen. In the center of the right wall is a window that is wooden, which opens outward on hinges. Downstage right is a small door leading off to a bedroom, and opposite, downstage left, another door leads out into the backyard, and on into the cotton fields beyond. There is also a smaller table and a cupboard against the wall. An old dresser stands against the right wall, between the window and the downstage door. There is a shelf on the left wall with a pail of drinking water, and a large tin dipper. Various cooking utensils, and items like salt and pepper, are scattered about in appropriate places.)

(At Rise: The curtain rises on a stage in semi-darkness. After a moment, when the lights have come up, the door in the up right corner bursts open: Enter **PURLIE JUDSON**. **PURLIE JUDSON** *is tall, restless, and commanding. In his middle or late thirties, he wears a wide-brim, ministerial black hat, a string tie, and a claw-hammer coat, which, though far from new, does not fit him too badly. His arms are loaded with large boxes and parcels, which must have come fresh from a department store.* **PURLIE** *is a man consumed with that divine impatience, without which nothing truly good, or truly bad, or even truly ridiculous, is ever accomplished in this world – with rhetoric and flourish to match.)*

PURLIE. *(Calling out loudly.)* Missy! *(No answer.)* Gitlow! – It's me – Purlie Victorious! *(Still no answer.* **PURLIE** *empties his overloaded arms, with obvious relief, on top of the big center table. He stands, mops his brow, and blows.)* Nobody home it seems. *(This last he says to someone he assumes has come in with him. When there is no answer he hurries to the door through which he entered.)* Come on – come on in!

(Enter **LUTIEBELLE JENKINS**, *slowly, as if bemused. Young, eager, well-built: though we cannot tell it at the moment. Clearly a girl from the backwoods, she carries a suitcase tied up with a rope in one hand, and a greasy shoebox with what's left of her lunch, together with an out-moded, out-sized handbag, in the other. Obviously she has traveled a great distance, but she still manages to look fresh and healthy. Her hat is a horror with feathers, but she wears it like a banner. Her shoes are flat-heeled and plain white, such as a good servant girl in the white folks' kitchen who*

*knows her place absolutely is bound to wear.
Her fall coat is dowdy, but well-intentioned
with a stingy strip of rabbit fur around the
neck.* **LUTIEBELLE** *is like thousands of Negro
girls you might know. Eager, desirous – even
anxious, keenly in search for life and for love,
trembling on the brink of self-confident and
vigorous young womanhood – but afraid to
take the final leap: because no one has ever
told her it is no longer necessary to be white in
order to be virtuous, charming, or beautiful.)*

LUTIEBELLE. *(Looking around as if at a museum of great
importance.)* Nobody home it seems.

PURLIE. *(Annoyed to find himself so exactly echoed,
looks at her sharply. He takes his watch from his vest
pocket, where he wears it on a chain.)* Cotton-picking
time in Georgia it's against the law to be home. Come
in – unload yourself. *(Crosses and looks out into the
kitchen.)*

> (**LUTIEBELLE** *is so enthralled, she still stands
> with all her bags and parcels in her arm.)*

Set your suitcase down.

LUTIEBELLE. What?

PURLIE. It's making you lopsided.

LUTIEBELLE. *(Snapping out of it.)* It is? I didn't even
notice. *(Sets suitcase, lunch box, and parcels down.)*

PURLIE. *(Studies her for a moment; goes and gently takes
off her hat.)* Tired?

LUTIEBELLE. Not stepping high as I am!

PURLIE. *(Takes the rest of her things and sets them on the
table.)* Hungry?

LUTIEBELLE. No, sir. But there's still some of my lunch left
if you –

PURLIE. *(Quickly.)* No, thank you. Two ham-hock sandwiches in one day is my limit. *(Sits down and fans himself with his hat.)* Sorry I had to walk you so far so fast.

LUTIEBELLE. *(Dreamily.)* Oh, I didn't mind, sir. Walking's good for you, Miz Emmylou sez –

PURLIE. Miz Emmylou can afford to say that: Miz Emmylou got a car. While all the transportation we got in the world is tied up in second-hand shoe leather. But never mind, my sister, never-you-mind! *(Rises, almost as if to dance, exaltation glowing in his eyes.)* And toll the bell, Big Bethel – toll that big, black, fat and sassy liberty bell! Tell Freedom the bridegroom cometh; the day of her deliverance is now at hand! (**PURLIE** *catches sight of* **MISSY** *through door down left.)* Oh, there she is. *(Crosses to door and calls out.)* Missy! – Oh, Missy!

MISSY. *(From a distance.)* Yes-s-s-s-!

PURLIE. It's me! – Purlie!

MISSY. Purlie Victorious?

PURLIE. Yes. Put that battling stick down and come on in here!

MISSY. All right!

PURLIE. *(Crosses hurriedly back to above table at center.)* That's Missy, my sister-in-law I was telling you about. *(Clears the table of everything but one of the large cartons, which he proceeds to open.)*

LUTIEBELLE. *(Not hearing him. Still awe-struck to be in the very house, in perhaps the very same room that* **PURLIE** *might have been born in.)* So this is the house where you was born and bred at.

PURLIE. Yep! Better'n being born outdoors.

LUTIEBELLE. What a lovely background for your home-life.

PURLIE. I wouldn't give it to my dog to raise fleas in!

LUTIEBELLE. So clean – and nice – and warm-hearted!

PURLIE. The first chance I get I'ma burn the damn thing down!

LUTIEBELLE. But – Reb'n Purlie! – It's yours, and that's what counts. Like Miz Emmylou scz –

PURLIE. Come here! *(Pulls her across to the window, flings it open.)* You see that big white house, perched on top of that hill with them two windows looking right down at us like two eyeballs: that's where Ol' Cap'n lives.

LUTIEBELLE. Ol' Cap'n?

PURLIE. Stonewall Jackson Cotchipee. He owns this dump, not me.

LUTIEBELLE. Oh –

PURLIE. And that ain't all: hill and dale, field and farm, truck and tractor, horse and mule, bird and bee and bush and tree – and cotton! – cotton by boll and by bale – every bit o' cotton you see in this county! – Everything and everybody he owns!

LUTIEBELLE. Everybody? You mean he owns people?

PURLIE. *(Bridling his impatience.)* Well – look! – ain't a man, woman or child working in this valley that ain't in debt to that ol' bastard! – *(Catches himself.)* bustard! – *(This still won't do.)* buzzard! – And that includes Gitlow and Missy – everybody – except me. –

LUTIEBELLE. But folks can't own people no more, Reb'n Purlie. Miz Emmylou sez that –

PURLIE. *(Verging on explosion.)* You ain't working for Miz Emmylou no more, you're working for me – Purlie Victorious. Freedom is my business, and I say that ol' man runs this plantation on debt: the longer you work for Ol' Cap'n Cotchipee, the more you owe at the commissary; and if you don't pay up, you can't leave. And I don't give a damn what Miz Emmylou nor nobody else sez – that's slavery!

LUTIEBELLE. I'm sorry, Reb'n Purlie –

PURLIE. Don't apologize, wait! – Just wait! – till I get my church; – wait till I buy Big Bethel back – *(Crosses to window and looks out.)* Wait till I stand once again in the pulpit of Grandpaw Kinkaid, and call upon my people – and talk to my people – About Ol' Cap'n, that miserable son-of-a–

LUTIEBELLE. *(Just in time to save him.)* Wait –!

PURLIE. Wait, I say! And we'll see who's gonna dominize this valley! – him or me! *(Turns and sees **MISSY** through door down left.)* Missy –!

> *(Enter **MISSY**, ageless, benign, and smiling. She wears a ragged old straw hat, a big house apron over her faded gingham, and low-cut, dragged-out tennis shoes on her feet. She is strong and of good cheer – of a certain shrewdness, yet full of the desire to believe. Her eyes light on **LUTIEBELLE**, and her arms go up and outward automatically.)*

MISSY. Purlie!

PURLIE. *(Thinks she is reaching for him.)* Missy!

MISSY. *(Ignoring him, clutching **LUTIEBELLE**, laughing and crying.)* Well – well – well!

PURLIE. *(Breaking the stranglehold.)* For God's sake, Missy, don't choke her to death!

MISSY. All my life – all my life I been praying for me a daughter just like you. My prayers is been answered at last. Welcome to our home, whoever you is!

LUTIEBELLE. *(Deeply moved.)* Thank you, ma'am.

MISSY. "Ma'am – ma'am." Listen to the child, Purlie. Everybody down here calls me Aunt Missy, and I'd be much obliged if you would, too.

LUTIEBELLE. It would make me very glad to do so – Aunt Missy.

MISSY. Uhmmmmmm! Pretty as a pan of buttermilk biscuits. Where on earth did you find her, Purlie? *(***PURLIE** *starts to answer.)* Let me take your things – now, you just make yourself at home – Are you hungry?

LUTIEBELLE. No, ma'am, but cheap as water is, I sure ain't got no business being this thirsty!

MISSY. *(Starts forward.)* I'll get some for you –

PURLIE. *(Intercepts her; directs* **LUTIEBELLE***.)* There's the dipper. And right out yonder by the fence just this side of that great big live oak tree you'll find the well – sweetest water in Cotchipee county.

LUTIEBELLE. Thank you, Reb'n Purlie. I'm very much obliged. *(Takes dipper from water pail and exits down left.)*

MISSY. Reb'n who?

PURLIE. *(Looking off after Lutiebelle.)* Perfection – absolute Ethiopian perfect. Hah, Missy?

MISSY. *(Looking off after Lutiebelle.)* Oh, I don't know about that.

PURLIE. What you mean you don't know? This girl looks more like Cousin Bee than Cousin Bee ever did.

MISSY. No resemblance to me.

PURLIE. Don't be ridiculous; she's the spitting image –

MISSY. No resemblance whatsoever!

PURLIE. I ought to know how my own cousin looked –

MISSY. But I was the last one to see her alive –

PURLIE. Twins, if not closer!

MISSY. Are you crazy? Bee was more lean, loose, and leggy –

PURLIE. Maybe so, but this girl makes it up in –

MISSY. With no chin to speak of – her eyes: sort of fickle one to another –

PURLIE. I know, but even so –

MISSY. *(Pointing off in Lutiebelle's direction.)* Look at her head – it ain't nearly as built like a rutabaga as Bee's own was!

PURLIE. *(Exasperated.)* What's the difference! White folks can't tell one of us from another by the head!

MISSY. Twenty years ago it was, Purlie, Ol' Cap'n laid bull whip to your natural behind –

PURLIE. Twenty years ago I swore I'd see his soul in hell!

MISSY. And I don't think you come full back to your senses yet – That ol' man ain't no fool!

PURLIE. That makes it one "no fool" against another.

MISSY. He's dangerous, Purlie. We could get killed if that old man was to find out what we was trying to do to get that church back.

PURLIE. How can he find out? Missy, how many times must I tell you, if it's one thing I am foolproof in it's white folks' psychology.

MISSY. That's exactly what I'm afraid of.

PURLIE. Freedom, Missy, that's what Big Bethel means. For you, me and Gitlow. And we can buy it for five hundred dollars, Missy. Freedom! – You want it, or don't you?

MISSY. Of course I want it, but – After all, Purlie, that rich ol' lady didn't exactly leave that five hundred dollars to us –

PURLIE. She left it to Aunt Henrietta –

MISSY. Aunt Henrietta is dead –

PURLIE. Exactly –

MISSY. And Henrietta's daughter Cousin Bee is dead, too.

PURLIE. Which makes us next in line to inherit the money by law!

MISSY. All right, then, why don't we just go on up that hill man-to-man and tell Ol' Cap'n we want our money?

PURLIE. Missy! You have been black as long as I have –

MISSY. *(Not above having her own little joke.)* Hell, boy, we could make him give it to us.

PURLIE. Make him – how? He's a white man, Missy. What you plan to do, sue him?

MISSY. *(Drops her teasing; thinks seriously for a moment.)* After all, it is our money. And it was our church.

PURLIE. And can you think of a better way to get it back than that girl out there?

MISSY. But you think it'll work, Purlie? You really think she can fool Ol' Cap'n?

PURLIE. He'll never know what hit him.

MISSY. Maybe – but there's still the question of Gitlow.

PURLIE. What about Gitlow?

MISSY. Gitlow has changed his mind.

PURLIE. Then you'll have to change it back.

GITLOW. *(Offstage.)* Help, Missy; help, Missy; help, Missy; help, Missy! *(***GITLOW** *runs on.)*

MISSY. What the devil's the matter this time?

GITLOW. There I was, Missy, picking in the high cotton, twice as fast as the human eye could see. All of a sudden I missed a boll and it fell – it fell on the ground, Missy! I stooped as fast as I could to pick it up and – *(He stoops to illustrate. There is a loud tearing of cloth.)* ripped the seat of my britches. There I was, Missy, exposed from stem to stern.

MISSY. What's so awful about that? It's only cotton.

GITLOW. But cotton is white, Missy. We must maintain respect. Bring me my Sunday School britches.

MISSY. What!

GITLOW. Ol' Cap'n is coming down into the cotton patch today, and I know you want your Gitlow to look his level best. (**MISSY** *starts to answer.*) Hurry, Missy, hurry! (**GITLOW** *hurries her off.*)

PURLIE. Gitlow – have I got the girl!

GITLOW. Is that so – what girl?

PURLIE. *(Taking him to the door.)* See? There she is! Well?

GITLOW. Well what?

PURLIE. What do you think?

GITLOW. Nope; she'll never do.

PURLIE. What you mean, she'll never do?

GITLOW. My advice to you is to take that girl back to Florida as fast as you can!

PURLIE. I can't take her back to Florida.

GITLOW. Why can't you take her back to Florida?

PURLIE. 'Cause she comes from Alabama. Gitlow, look at her: she's just the size – just the type – just the style.

GITLOW. And just the girl to get us all in jail. The answer is no! *(Crosses to kitchen door.)* MISSY! *(Back to* **PURLIE**.*)* Girl or no girl, I ain't getting mixed up in no more of your nightmares – I got my own. Dammit, Missy, I said let's go!

MISSY. *(Entering with trousers.)* You want me to take my bat to you again?

GITLOW. No, Missy, control yourself. It's just that every second Gitlow's off the firing line-up, seven pounds of

Ol' Cap'n's cotton don't git gotten. *(Snatches pants from* **MISSY**, *but is in too much of a hurry to put them on – starts off.)*

PURLIE. Wait a minute, Gitlow... Wait!

*(**GITLOW** is off in a flash.)*

Missy! Stop him!

MISSY. He ain't as easy to stop as he used to be. Especially now Ol' Cap'n's made him Deputy-For-The-Colored.

PURLIE. Deputy-For-The-Colored? What the devil is that?

MISSY. Who knows? All I know is Gitlow's changed his mind.

PURLIE. But Gitlow can't change his mind!

MISSY. Oh, it's easy enough when you ain't got much to start with. I warned you. You don't know how shifty ol' Git can git. He's the hardest man to convince and keep convinced I ever seen in my life.

PURLIE. Missy, you've got to make him go up that hill, he's got to identify this girl – Ol' Cap'n won't believe nobody else.

MISSY. I know –

PURLIE. He's got to swear before Ol' Cap'n that this girl is the real Cousin Bee –

MISSY. I know.

PURLIE. Missy, you're the only person in this world ol' Git'll really listen to.

MISSY. I know.

PURLIE. And what if you do have to hit him a time or two – it's for his own good!

MISSY. I know.

PURLIE. He'll recover from it, Missy. He always does –

MISSY. I know.

PURLIE. Freedom, Missy – Big Bethel; for you; me; and Gitlow –!

MISSY. Freedom – and a little something left over – that's all I ever wanted all my life. *(Looks out into the yard.)* She do look a little somewhat like Cousin Bee – about the feet!

PURLIE. Of course she does –

MISSY. I won't guarantee nothing, Purlie – but I'll try.

PURLIE. *(Grabbing her and dancing her around.)* Everytime I see you, Missy, you get prettier by the pound!

>   (**LUTIEBELLE** *enters.* **MISSY** *sees her.)*

MISSY. Stop it, Purlie, stop it! Stop it. Quit cutting the fool in front of company!

PURLIE. *(Sees* **LUTIEBELLE***, crosses to her, grabs her about the waist and swings her around too.)*
How wondrous are the daughters of my people,
Yet knoweth not the glories of themselves!

> *(Spins her around for* **MISSY***'s inspection. She does look better with her coat off, in her immaculate blue and white maid's uniform.)*

Where do you suppose I found her, Missy –
This Ibo prize – this Zulu Pearl –
This long lost lily of the black Mandingo –
Kikuyu maid, beneath whose brown embrace
Hot suns of Africa are burning still: where – where?
A drudge; a serving wench; a feudal fetch-pot:
A common scullion in the white man's kitchen.
Drowned is her youth in thankless Southern dishpans;
Her beauty spilt for Dixiecratic pigs!
This brown-skinned grape! this wine of Negro vintage –

MISSY. *(Interrupting.)* I know all that, Purlie, but what's her name?

> (**PURLIE** *looks at* **LUTIEBELLE** *and turns abruptly away.*)

LUTIEBELLE. I don't think he likes my name so much – it's Lutiebelle, ma'am – Lutiebelle Gussiemae Jenkins!

MISSY. *(Gushing with motherly reassurance.)* Lutiebelle Gussiemae Jenkins! My, that's nice.

PURLIE. Nice! It's an insult to the Negro people!

MISSY. Purlie, behave yourself!

PURLIE. A previous condition of servitude, a badge of inferiority, and I refuse to have it in my organization! – change it!

MISSY. You want me to box your mouth for you!

PURLIE. Lutiebelle Gussiemae Jenkins! What does it mean in Swahili? Cheap labor!

LUTIEBELLE. Swahili?

PURLIE. One of the thirteen silver tongues of Africa: Swahili, Bushengo, Ashanti, Baganda, Herero, Yoruba, Bambora, Mpongwe, Swahili: a language of moons, of velvet drums; hot days of rivers, red-splashed, and bird-song bright!, black fingers in rice white at sunset red! – ten thousand Queens of Sheba –*

MISSY. *(Having to interrupt.)* Just where did Purlie find you, honey?

LUTIEBELLE. It was in Dothan, Alabama, last Sunday, Aunt Missy, right in the junior choir!

MISSY. The junior choir – my, my, my!

---

* While Purlie claims there are "thirteen silver tongues of Africa," he names only eight – mispronouncing three (Bushongo, Luganda, Bambara). This mispronunciation is a deliberate choice by the playwright.

PURLIE. *(Still carried away.)*
Behold! I said, this dark and holy vessel,
In whom should burn that golden nut-brown joy
Which Negro womanhood was meant to be.
Ten thousand queens, ten thousand Queens of Sheba:

   *(Pointing at **LUTIEBELLE**.)*

Ethiopia herself – in all her beauteous wonder,
Come to restore the ancient thrones of Cush!

MISSY. Great Gawdamighty, Purlie, I can't hear myself think –!

LUTIEBELLE. That's just what I said last Sunday, Aunt Missy, when Reb'n Purlie started preaching that thing in the pulpit.

MISSY. Preaching it?!

LUTIEBELLE. Lord, Aunt Missy, I shouted clear down to the Mourners' Bench.

MISSY. *(To **PURLIE**.)* But last time you was a professor of Negro Philosophy.

PURLIE. I told you, Missy: my intention is to buy Big Bethel back; to reclaim the ancient pulpit of Grandpaw Kincaid, and preach freedom in the cotton patch – I told you!

MISSY. Maybe you did, Purlie, maybe you did. You got yourself a license?

PURLIE. Naw! – but –

MISSY. *(Looking him over.)* Purlie Victorious Judson: Self-made minister of the gospel – claw-hammer coattail, shoe-string tie and all.

PURLIE. *(Quietly but firmly holding his ground.)* How else can you lead the Negro people?

MISSY. Is that what you got in your mind: leading the Negro people?

PURLIE. Who else is they got?

MISSY. God help the race.

LUTIEBELLE. It was a sermon, I mean, Aunt Missy, the likes of which has never been heard before.

MISSY. Oh, I bet that. Tell me about it, son. What did you preach?

PURLIE. I preached the New Baptism of Freedom for all mankind, according to the Declaration of Independence, taking as my text the Constitution of the United States of America, Amendments First through Fifteenth, which readeth as follows: "Congress shall make no law –"

MISSY. Enough – that's enough, son – I'm converted. But it is confusing, all the changes you keep going through. *(To* **LUTIEBELLE**.*)* Honey, every time I see Purlie he's somebody else.

PURLIE. Not any more, Missy; and if I'm lying may the good Lord put me down in the book of bad names: Purlie is put forever!

MISSY. Yes. But will he stay put forever?

PURLIE. There is in every man a finger of iron that points him what he must and must not do –

MISSY. And your finger points up the hill to that five hundred dollars with which you'll buy Big Bethel back, preach freedom in the cotton patch, and live happily ever after!

PURLIE. The soul-consuming passion of my life! *(Draws out watch.)* It's two fifteen, Missy, and Gitlow's waiting. Missy, I suggest you get a move on.

MISSY. I already got a move on. Had it since four o'clock this morning!

PURLIE. Time, Missy – exactly what the colored man in this country ain't got, and you're wasting it!

MISSY. *(Looks at* **PURLIE**, *and decides not to strike him dead.)* Purlie, would you mind stepping out into the cotton patch and telling your brother Gitlow I'd like a few words with him?

> *(***PURLIE**, *overjoyed, leaps at* **MISSY** *as if to hug and dance her around again, but she is too fast.)*

Do like I tell you now – go on!

> *(***PURLIE** *exits singing.)*

*(***MISSY** *turns to* **LUTIEBELLE** *to begin the important task of sizing her up.)* Besides, it wouldn't be hospitable not to set and visit a spell with our distinguished guest over from Dothan, Alabama.

LUTIEBELLE. *(This is the first time she has been called anything of importance by anybody.)* Thank you, ma'am.

MISSY. Now. Let's you and me just set back and enjoy a piece of my potato pie. You like potato pie, don't you?

LUTIEBELLE. Oh, yes, ma'am, I like it very much.

MISSY. And get real acquainted. *(Offers her a saucer with a slice of pie on it.)*

LUTIEBELLE. I'm ever so much obliged. My, this looks nice! Uhm, uhn, uhn!

MISSY. *(Takes a slice for herself and sits down.)* You know – ever since that ol' man – *(Indicates up the hill.)* took after Purlie so unmerciful with that bull whip twenty years ago – he fidgets! Always on the go; rattling around from place to place all over the country: one step ahead of the white folks – something about Purlie always did irritate the white folks.

LUTIEBELLE. Is that the truth!

MISSY. Oh, my yes. Finally wound up being locked up a time or two for safekeeping –

> (**LUTIEBELLE** *parts with a loud, sympathetic grunt.*)

(Changing her tack a bit.) Always kept up his schooling, though. In fact that boy's got one of the best second-hand educations in this country.

LUTIEBELLE. *(Brightening considerably.)* Is that a fact!

MISSY. Used to read everything he could get his hands on.

LUTIEBELLE. He did? Ain't that wonderful!

MISSY. Till one day he finally got tired, and throwed all his books to the hogs – not enough "Negro" in them, he said. After that he puttered around with first one thing then another. Remember that big bus boycott they had in Montgomery? Well, we don't travel by bus in the cotton patch, so Purlie boycotted mules!

LUTIEBELLE. You don't say so?

MISSY. Another time he invented a secret language, that Negroes could understand but white folks couldn't.

LUTIEBELLE. Oh, my goodness gracious!

MISSY. He sent it C.O.D. to the NAACP but they never answered his letter.

LUTIEBELLE. Oh, they will, Aunt Missy; you can just bet your life they will.

MISSY. I don't mind it so much. Great leaders are bound to pop up from time to time 'mongst our people – in fact we sort of look forward to it. But Purlie's in such a hurry I'm afraid he'll lose his mind.

LUTIEBELLE. Lose his mind – no! Oh, no!

MISSY. That is unless you and me can do something about it.

LUTIEBELLE. You and me? Do what, Aunt Missy? You tell me – I'll do anything!

MISSY. *(Having found all she needs to know.)* Well, now; ain't nothing ever all that peculiar about a man a good wife – and a family – and some steady home cooking won't cure. Don't you think so?

LUTIEBELLE. *(Immensely relieved.)* Oh, yes, Aunt Missy, yes. *(But still not getting* **MISSY**'s *intent.)* You'd be surprised how many tall, good-looking, great big, ol' handsome looking mens – just like Reb'n Purlie – walking around, starving theyselves to death! Oh, I just wish I had one to aim my pot at!

MISSY. Well, Purlie Judson is the uncrowned appetite of the age.

LUTIEBELLE. He is! What's his favorite?

MISSY. Anything! Anything a fine-looking, strong and healthy – girl like you could put on the table.

LUTIEBELLE. Like me? Like ME! Oh, Aunt Missy –!

MISSY. *(Purlie's future is settled.)* Honey, I mind once at the Sunday School picnic Purlie et a whole sack o' pullets!

LUTIEBELLE. Oh, I just knowed there was something – something – just reeks about that man. He puts me in the mind of all the good things I ever had in my life. Picnics, fish-fries, corn-shuckings, and love-feasts, and gospel-singings – picking huckleberries, roasting groundpeas, quilting-bee parties and barbecues; that certain kind of – welcome – you can't get nowhere else in all this world. Aunt Missy, life is so good to us – sometimes!

MISSY. Oh, child, being colored can be a lotta fun when ain't nobody looking.

LUTIEBELLE. Ain't it the truth! I always said I'd never pass for white, no matter how much they offered me, unless the things I love could pass, too.

MISSY. Ain't it the beautiful truth!

*(***PURLIE*** enters again; agitated.)*

PURLIE. Missy – Gitlow says if you want him come and get him!

MISSY. *(Rises, crosses to door down left; looks out.)* Lawd, that man do take his cotton picking seriously. *(Comes back to **LUTIEBELLE** and takes her saucer.)* Did you get enough to eat, honey?

LUTIEBELLE. Indeed I did. And Aunt Missy, I haven't had potato pie like that since the senior choir give –

MISSY. *(Still ignoring **PURLIE**.)* That's where I met Gitlow, you know. On the senior choir.

LUTIEBELLE. Aunt Missy! I didn't know you could sing!

MISSY. Like a brown-skin nightingale. Well, it was a Sunday afternoon – Big Bethel had just been –

PURLIE. Dammit, Missy! The white man is five hundred years ahead of us in this country, and we ain't gonna ever gonna catch up with him sitting around on our non-Caucasian rumps talking about the senior choir!

MISSY. *(Starts to bridle at this sudden display of passion, but changes her mind.)* Right this way, honey. *(Heads for door down right.)* Where Cousin Bee used to sleep at.

LUTIEBELLE. Yes, ma'am. *(Starts to follow **MISSY**.)*

PURLIE. *(Stopping her.)* Wait a minute – don't forget your clothes! *(Gives her a large carton.)*

MISSY. It ain't much, the roof leaks, and you can get as much September inside as you can outside any time; but I try to keep it clean.

PURLIE. Cousin Bee was known for her clothes!

MISSY. Stop nagging, Purlie – *(To **LUTIEBELLE**.)* There's plenty to eat in the kitchen.

LUTIEBELLE. Thank you, Aunt Missy. *(Exits down right.)*

PURLIE. *(Following after her.)* And hurry! We want to leave as soon as Missy gets Gitlow in from the cotton patch!

MISSY. *(Blocking his path.)* Mr. Preacher – *(She pulls him out of earshot.)* If we do pull this thing off – *(Studying him a moment.)* what do you plan to do with her after that – send her back where she came from?

PURLIE. Dothan, Alabama? Never! Missy, there a million things I can do with a girl like that, right here in Big Bethel!

MISSY. Yeah! Just make sure they're all legitimate. Anyway, marriage is still cheap, and we can always use another cook in the family!

> *(**PURLIE** hasn't the slightest idea what **MISSY** is talking about.)*

LUTIEBELLE. *(From offstage.)* Aunt Missy.

MISSY. Yes, honey.

LUTIEBELLE. *(Offstage.)* Whose picture is this on the dresser?

MISSY. Why, that's Cousin Bee.

LUTIEBELLE. *(A moment's silence. Then she enters hastily, carrying a large photograph in her hand.)* Cousin Bee!

MISSY. Yes, poor thing. She's the one the whole thing is all about.

LUTIEBELLE. *(The edge of panic.)* Cousin Bee – Oh, my! – Oh, my goodness! My goodness gracious!

MISSY. What's the matter?

LUTIEBELLE. But she's pretty – she's so pretty!

MISSY. *(Takes photograph; looks at it tenderly.)* Yes – she was pretty. I guess they took this shortly before she died.

LUTIEBELLE. And you mean – you want me to look like her?

PURLIE. That's the idea. Now go and get into your clothes. *(Starts to push her off.)*

MISSY. They sent it down to us from the college. Don't she look smart? I'll bet she was a good student when she was living.

LUTIEBELLE. *(Evading* **PURLIE**.*)* Good student!

MISSY. Yes. One more year and she'd have finished.

LUTIEBELLE. Oh, my gracious Lord have mercy upon my poor soul!

PURLIE. *(Not appreciating her distress or its causes.)* Awake, awake! Put on thy strength, O, Zion – put on thy beautiful garments. *(Hurries her offstage.)* And hurry! *(Turning to* **MISSY**.*)* Missy, Big Bethel and Gitlow is waiting. Grandpaw Kincaid gave his life. *(Gently places the bat into her hand.)* It is a far greater thing you do now, than you've ever done before – and Gitlow ain't never got his head knocked off in a better cause.

> *(***MISSY*** *nods her head in sad agreement, and accepts the bat.* **PURLIE** *helps her to the door down left, where she exits, a most reluctant executioner.* **PURLIE** *stands and watches her off from the depth of his satisfaction. The door down right eases open, and* **LUTIEBELLE**, *her suitcase, handbag, fall coat, and lunch box firmly in hand, tries to sneak out the front door.* **PURLIE** *hears her, and turns just in time.)*

Where do you think you're going?

LUTIEBELLE. Did you see that, Reb'n Purlie? *(Indicating bedroom from which she just came.)* Did you see all them beautiful clothes – slips, hats, shoes, stockings? I mean nylon stockings like Miz Emmylou wears – and a dress, like even Miz Emmylou don't wear. Did you look at what was in that big box?

PURLIE. Of course I looked at what was in that big box – I bought it – all of it – for you.

LUTIEBELLE. For me!

PURLIE. Of course! I told you! And as soon as we finish you can have it!

LUTIEBELLE. Reb'n Purlie, I'm a good girl. I ain't never done nothing in all this world, white, colored or otherwise, to hurt nobody!

PURLIE. I know that.

LUTIEBELLE. I work hard; I mop, I scrub, I iron; I'm clean and polite, and I know how to get along with white folks' children better'n they do. I pay my church dues every second and fourth Sunday the Lord sends; and I can cook catfish – and hushpuppies – You like hushpuppies, don't you, Reb'n Purlie?

PURLIE. I love hushpuppies!

LUTIEBELLE. Hushpuppies – and corn dodgers; I can cook you a corn dodger would give you the swimming in the head!

PURLIE. I'm sure you can, but –

LUTIEBELLE. But I ain't never been in a mess like this in all my life!

PURLIE. Mess – what mess?

LUTIEBELLE. You mean go up that hill, in all them pretty clothes, and pretend – in front of white folks – that – that I'm your Cousin Bee – somebody I ain't never seen or heard of before in my whole life!

PURLIE. Why not? Some of the best pretending in the world is done in front of white folks.

LUTIEBELLE. But Reb'n Purlie, I didn't know your Cousin Bee was a student at the college; I thought she worked there!

PURLIE. But I told you on the train –

LUTIEBELLE. Don't do no good to tell ME nothing, Reb'n Purlie! I never listen. Ask Miz Emmylou and 'em, they'll tell you I never listen. I didn't know it was a college lady you wanted me to make like. I thought it was for a sleep-in like me. I thought all that stuff you bought in them boxes was stuff for maids and cooks and – Why, I ain't never even been near a college!

PURLIE. So what? College ain't so much where you been as how you talk when you get back. Anybody can do it; look at me.

LUTIEBELLE. Nawsir, I think you better look at me like Miz Emmylou sez –

PURLIE. *(Taking her by the shoulders, tenderly.)* Calm down – just take it easy, and calm down.

> *(She subsides a little, her chills banished by the warmth of him.)*

Now – don't tell me, after all that big talking you done on the train about white folks, you're scared.

LUTIEBELLE. Talking big is easy – from the proper distance.

PURLIE. Why – don't you believe in yourself?

LUTIEBELLE. Some.

PURLIE. Don't you believe in your own race of people?

LUTIEBELLE. Oh, yessir – a little.

PURLIE. Don't you believe the black man is coming to power some day?

LUTIEBELLE. Almost.

PURLIE. Ten thousand Queens of Sheba! What kind of a Negro are you! Where's your race pride?

LUTIEBELLE. Oh, I'm a great one for race pride, sir, believe me – it's just that I don't need it much in my line of work! Miz Emmylou sez –

PURLIE. Damn Miz Emmylou! Does her blond hair and blue eyes make her any more of a woman in the sight of her men folks than your black hair and brown eyes in mine?

LUTIEBELLE. No, sir!

PURLIE. Is her lily-white skin any more money-under-the-mattress than your fine fair brown? And if so, why does she spend half her life at the beach trying to get a sun tan?

LUTIEBELLE. I never thought of that!

PURLIE. There's a whole lotta things about the Negro question you ain't thought of! The South is split like a fat man's underwear; and somebody beside the Supreme Court has got to make a stand for the everlasting glory of our people!

LUTIEBELLE. Yessir.

PURLIE. Snatch Freedom from the jaws of force and filibuster!

LUTIEBELLE. Amen to that!

PURLIE. Put thunder in the Senate –!

LUTIEBELLE. Yes, Lord!

PURLIE. And righteous indignation back in the halls of Congress!

LUTIEBELLE. Ain't it the truth!

PURLIE. Make Civil Rights from Civil Wrongs; and bring that ol' Civil War to a fair and a just conclusion!

LUTIEBELLE. Help him, Lord!

PURLIE. Remind this white and wicked world there ain't been more'n a dime's worth of difference twixt one man and another'n, irregardless of race, gender, creed, or color – since God Himself Almighty set the first batch

out to dry before the chimneys of Zion got hot! The
eyes and ears of the world is on Big Bethel!

LUTIEBELLE. Amen and hallelujah!

PURLIE. And whose side are you fighting on this evening,
sister?

LUTIEBELLE. Great Gawdamighty, Reb'n Purlie, on the
Lord's side! But Miz Emmylou sez –

PURLIE. *(Blowing up.)* This is outrageous – this is a
catastrophe! You're a disgrace to the Negro profession!

LUTIEBELLE. That's just what she said all right – her
exactly words.

PURLIE. Who's responsible for this? Where's your Maw
and Paw at?

LUTIEBELLE. I reckon I ain't rightly got no Maw and Paw,
wherever they at.

PURLIE. What!

LUTIEBELLE. And nobody else that I knows of. You see,
sir – I been on the go from one white folks' kitchen to
another since before I can remember. How I got there
in the first place – whatever became of my Maw and
Paw, and my kin folks – even what my real name is –
nobody is ever rightly said.

PURLIE. *(Genuinely touched.)* Oh. A motherless child –

LUTIEBELLE. That's what Miz Emmylou always sez –

PURLIE. But – who cared for you – like a mother? Who
brung you up – who raised you?

LUTIEBELLE. Nobody in particular – just whoever
happened to be in charge of the kitchen that day.

PURLIE. That explains the whole thing – no wonder; you've
missed the most important part of being somebody.

LUTIEBELLE. I have? What part is that?

PURLIE. Love – being appreciated, and sought out, and looked after; being fought to the bitter end over even.

LUTIEBELLE. Oh, I have missed that, Reb'n Purlie, I really have. Take mens – all my life they never looked at me the way other girls get looked at!

PURLIE. That's not so. The very first time I saw you – right up there in the junior choir – I give you that look!

LUTIEBELLE. *(Turning to him in absolute ecstasy.)* You did! Oh, I thought so! – I prayed so. All through your sermon I thought I would faint from hoping so hard so. Oh, Reb'n Purlie – I think that's the finest look a person could ever give a person – Oh, Reb'n Purlie! *(She closes her eyes and points her lips at him.)*

PURLIE. *(Starts to kiss her, but draws back shyly.)* Lutiebelle –

LUTIEBELLE. *(Dreamily, her eyes still closed.)* Yes, Reb'n Purlie –

PURLIE. There's something I want to ask you – something I never – in all my life – thought I'd be asking a woman – Would you – I don't know exactly how to say it – would you –

LUTIEBELLE. Yes, Reb'n Purlie?

PURLIE. Would you be my disciple?

LUTIEBELLE. *(Rushing into his arms.)* Oh, yes, Reb'n Purlie, yes!

> *(They start to kiss, but are interrupted by a noise coming from offstage.)*

GITLOW. *(Offstage; in the extremity of death.)* No, Missy. No – no! – NO! –

> *(This last plea is choked off by the sound of some solid object brought smartly into contact with sudden flesh. "CLUNK!"* **PURLIE**

and **LUTIEBELLE** *stand looking off left, frozen for the moment.)*

LUTIEBELLE. *(Finally daring to speak.)* Oh, my Lord, Reb'n Purlie, what happened?

PURLIE. Gitlow has changed his mind. *(Grabs her and swings her around bodily.)* Toll the bell, Big Bethel! – toll that big, fat, black and sassy liberty bell. Tell Freedom –

*(***LUTIEBELLE*** suddenly leaps from the floor into his arms and plants her lips squarely on his. When finally he can come up for air.)*

Tell Freedom – tell Freedom – WOW!

Curtain

Scene Two

(Time: It is a little later the same afternoon.)

(Scene: We are now in the little business office off from the commissary, where all the inhabitants of Cotchipee Valley buy food, clothing, and supplies. In the back a traveler has been drawn with just enough of an opening left to serve as the door to the main part of the store. On stage left and on stage right are simulated shelves where various items of reserve stock are kept: A wash tub, an axe, sacks of peas, and flour; bolts of gingham and calico, etc. Downstage right is a small desk, on which an ancient typewriter and an adding machine, with various papers and necessary books and records of commerce, are placed. There is a small chair at this desk. Downstage left is a table, with a large cash register, that has a functioning drawer. Below this is an entrance from the street.)

(At Rise: As the curtain rises, a young white man of twenty-five or thirty, but still gawky, awkward, and adolescent in outlook and behavior, is sitting on a high stool downstage right center. His face is held in the hands of **IDELLA***, a Negro cook and woman of all work, who has been in the family since time immemorial. She is the only mother* **CHARLIE***, who is very much oversized even for his age, has ever known.* **IDELLA** *is as little as she is old and as tough as she is tiny, and is busily applying medication to* **CHARLIE***'s black eye.)*

CHARLIE. Ow, Idella, ow! – Ow!

IDELLA. Hold still, boy.

CHARLIE. But it hurts, Idella.

IDELLA. I know it hurts. Whoever done this to you musta meant to knock your natural brains out.

CHARLIE. I already told you who done it – OW!

IDELLA. Charlie Cotchipee, if you don't hold still and let me put this hot poultice on your eye, you better!

> (**CHARLIE** *subsides and meekly accepts her ministrations.)*

First the milking, then the breakfast, then the dishes, then the washing, then the scrubbing, then the lunch time, next the dishes, then the ironing – and now; just where the picking and plucking for supper ought to be – you!

CHARLIE. You didn't tell Paw?

IDELLA. Of course I didn't – but the sheriff did.

CHARLIE. *(Leaping up.)* The sheriff!

IDELLA. *(Pushing him back down.)* Him and the deputy come to the house less than a hour ago.

CHARLIE. *(Leaping up again.)* Are they coming over here!

IDELLA. Of course they're coming over here – sooner or later.

CHARLIE. But what will I do, Idella, what will I say?

IDELLA. *(Pushing him down.* **CHARLIE** *subsides.)* "He that keepeth his mouth keepeth his life –"

CHARLIE. Did they ask for me?

IDELLA. Of course they asked for you.

CHARLIE. What did they say?

IDELLA. I couldn't hear too well; your father took them into the study and locked the door behind them.

CHARLIE. Maybe it was about something else.

IDELLA. It was about YOU: that much I could hear! Charlie – you want to get us both killed!

CHARLIE. I'm sorry, Idella, but –

IDELLA. *(Overriding; finishing proverb she had begun.)* "But he that openeth wide his lips shall have destruction!

CHARLIE. But it was you who said it was the law of the land –

IDELLA. I know I did –

CHARLIE. It was you who said it's got to be obeyed –

IDELLA. I know it was me, but –

CHARLIE. It was you who said everybody had to stand up and take a stand against –

IDELLA. I know it was me, dammit! But I didn't say take a stand in no barroom!

CHARLIE. Ben started it, not me. And you always said never to take low from the likes of him!

IDELLA. Not so loud; they may be out there in the commissary! *(Goes quickly to door up center and peers out; satisfied no one has overheard them she crosses back down to* **CHARLIE.***)* Look, boy, everybody down here don't feel as friendly towards the Supreme Court as you and me do – you big enough to know that! And don't you ever go outta here and pull a fool trick like you done last night again and not let me know about it in advance. You hear me!

CHARLIE. I'm sorry.

IDELLA. When you didn't come to breakfast this morning, and I went upstairs looking for you, and you just setting there, looking at me with your big eyes, and I seen that they had done hurt you – my, my, my! Whatever happens to you happens to me – you big enough to know that!

CHARLIE. I didn't mean to make trouble, Idella.

IDELLA. I know that, son, I know it. *(Makes final adjustments to the poultice.)* Now. No matter what happens when they do come I'll be right behind you. Keep your nerves calm and your mouth shut. Understand?

CHARLIE. Yes.

IDELLA. And as soon as you get a free minute come over to the house and let me put another hot poultice on that eye.

CHARLIE. Thank you, I'm very much obliged to you. Idella –

IDELLA. What is it, son?

CHARLIE. Sometimes I think I ought to run away from home.

IDELLA. I know, but you already tried that, honey.

CHARLIE. Sometimes I think I ought to run away from home – again!

> *(**OL' CAP'N** has entered from the commissary just in time to hear this last remark.)*

OL' CAP'N. Why don't you, boy – why don't you?

> *(**OL' CAP'N COTCHIPEE** is aged and withered a bit, but by no means infirm. Dressed in traditional southern linen, the wide hat, the shoestring tie, the long coat, the twirling moustache of the Ol' Southern Colonel. In his left hand he carries a cane, and in his right a coiled bull whip: his last line of defense. He stops long enough to establish the fact that he means business, threatens them both with a mean cantankerous eye, then hangs his whip – the definitive answer to all who might foolishly question his Confederate power and glory – upon a peg. **CHARLIE** freezes at the sound of his voice. **IDELLA** tenses but keeps working on **CHARLIE**'s eye. **OL' CAP'N** crosses*

down, rudely pushes her hand aside, lifts up **CHARLIE***'s chin so that he may examine the damage, shakes his head in disgust.)*

OL' CAP'N. You don't know, boy, what a strong stomach it takes to stomach you. Just look at you, sitting there – all slopped over like something the horses dropped; steam, stink and all!

IDELLA. Don't you dare talk like that to this child!

OL' CAP'N. *(This stops him – momentarily.)* When I think of his grandpaw, God rest his Confederate soul, hero of the battle of Chickamauga – *(It's too much.)* Get outta my sight!

> *(***CHARLIE*** *gets up to leave.)*

Not you – you! *(Indicates* **IDELLA***.)*

> *(She gathers up her things in silence and starts to leave.)*

Wait a minute – *(***IDELLA*** *stops.)* You been closer to this boy than I have, even before his ma died – ain't a thought ever entered his head you didn't know 'bout it first. You got anything to do with what my boy's been thinking lately?

IDELLA. I didn't know he had been thinking lately.

OL' CAP'N. Don't play with me, Idella – and you know what I mean! Who's been putting these integrationary ideas in my boy's head? Was it you – I'm asking you a question, dammit! Was it you?

IDELLA. Why don't you ask him?

OL' CAP'N. *(Snorts.)* Ask him! ASK HIM! He ain't gonna say a word unless you tell him to, and you know it. I'm asking you again, Idella Landy, have you been talking integration to my boy?!

IDELLA. I can't rightly answer you any more on that than he did.

OL' CAP'N. By God, you will answer me. I'll make you stand right there – right there! – all day and all night long, till you do answer me!

IDELLA. That's just fine.

OL' CAP'N. What's that! What's that you say?

IDELLA. I mean I ain't got nothing else to do – supper's on the stove; rice is ready, okra's fried, turnip's simmered, biscuits' baked, and stew is stewed. In fact them lemon pies you wanted special for supper are in the oven right now, just getting ready to burn –

OL' CAP'N. Get outta here!

IDELLA. Oh – no hurry, Ol' Cap'n –

OL' CAP'N. Get the hell out of here!

> (**IDELLA** *deliberately takes all the time in the world to pick up her things.*)

(Following her around trying to make his point.) I'm warning both of you; that little lick over the eye is a small skimption compared to what I'm gonna do. *(**IDELLA** pretends not to listen.)* I won't stop till I get to the bottom of this! *(**IDELLA** still ignores him.)* Get outta here, Idella Landy, before I take my cane and –

> (*He raises his cane but* **IDELLA** *insists on moving at her own pace to exit down left.*)

And save me some buttermilk to go with them lemon pies, you hear me! *(Turns to **CHARLIE**; not knowing how to approach him.)* The sheriff was here this morning.

CHARLIE. Yessir.

OL' CAP'N. Is that all you got to say to me: "Yessir"?

CHARLIE. Yessir.

OL' CAP'N. You are a disgrace to the southland!

CHARLIE. Yessir.

OL' CAP'N. Shut up! I could kill you, boy, you understand that? Kill you with my own two hands!

CHARLIE. Yessir.

OL' CAP'N. Shut up! I could beat you to death with that bull whip – put my pistol to your good-for-nothing head – my own flesh and blood – and blow your blasted brains all over this valley! *(Fighting to retain his control.)* If – if you wasn't the last living drop of Cotchipee blood in Cotchipee County, I'd – I'd –

CHARLIE. Yessir.

> *(This is too much.* **OL' CAP'N** *snatches* **CHARLIE** *to his feet. But* **CHARLIE** *does not resist.)*

OL' CAP'N. You trying to get non-violent with me, boy?

> *(***CHARLIE** *does not answer, just dangles there.)*

CHARLIE. *(Finally.)* I'm ready with the books, sir – that is – whenever you're ready.

OL' CAP'N. *(Flinging* **CHARLIE** *into a chair.)* Thank you – thank you! What with your Yankee propaganda, your barroom brawls, and all your other non-Confederate activities, I didn't think you had the time.

CHARLIE. *(Picks up account book; reads.)* "Cotton report. Fifteen bales picked yesterday and sent to the cotton gin; bringing our total to 357 bales to date."

OL' CAP'N. *(Impressed.)* 357 – boy, that's some picking. Who's ahead?

CHARLIE. Gitlow Judson, with seventeen bales up to now.

OL' CAP'N. Gitlow Judson; well I'll be damned; did you ever see a cotton-pickinger darky in your whole life?!

CHARLIE. Commissary report –

OL' CAP'N. Did you ever look down into the valley and watch ol' Git a-picking his way through that cotton patch? Holy Saint Mother's Day! I'll bet you –

CHARLIE. Commissary report!

OL' CAP'N. All right! – commissary report.

CHARLIE. Yessir – well, first, sir, there's been some complaints: the flour is spoiled, the beans are rotten, and the meat is tainted.

OL' CAP'N. Cut the price on it.

CHARLIE. But it's also a little wormy –

OL' CAP'N. Then sell it to the Negras – Is something wrong?

CHARLIE. No, sir – I mean, sir…, we can't go on doing that, sir.

OL' CAP'N. Why not? It's traditional.

CHARLIE. Yessir, but times are changing – all this debt – *(Indicates book.)* According to this book every family in this valley owes money they'll never be able to pay back.

OL' CAP'N. Of course – it's the only way to keep 'em working. Didn't they teach you nothin' at school?

CHARLIE. We're cheating them – and they know we're cheating them. How long do you expect them to stand for it?

OL' CAP'N. As long as they're Negras –

CHARLIE. How long before they start a-rearing up on their hind legs, and saying: "Enough, white folks – now that's enough! Either you start treating me like I'm somebody in this world, or I'll blow your brains out"?

OL' CAP'N. *(Shaken to the core.)* Stop it – stop it! You're tampering with the economic foundation of the southland! Are you trying to ruin me? One more word like that and I'll kill – I'll shoot – *(**CHARLIE** attempts* *to answer.)* Shut up! One more word and I'll – I'll fling myself on your Maw's grave and die of apoplexy. I'll –! I'll –! Shut up, do you hear me? Shut up!

> *(Enter* **GITLOW**, *hat in hand, grin on face, more obsequious today than ever.)*

Now what the hell *you* want?

GITLOW. *(Taken aback.)* Nothing, sir, nothing! – That is – Missy, my ol' 'oman – well, suh, to git to the truth of the matter, I got a little business –

OL' CAP'N. Negras ain't got no business. And if you don't get the hell back into that cotton patch you better. Git, I said!

> *(***GITLOW** *starts to beat a hasty retreat.)*

Oh, no – don't go. Uncle Gitlow – good ol' faithful ol' Gitlow. Don't go – don't go.

GITLOW. *(Not quite sure.)* Well – you're the boss, boss.

OL' CAP'N. *(Shoving a cigar into* **GITLOW**'*s mouth.)* Just the other day, I was talking to the Senator about you – What's that great big knot on your head?

GITLOW. Missy – I mean, a mosquito!

OL' CAP'N. *(In all seriousness, examining the bump.)* Uh! Musta been wearin' brass knuck – And he was telling me, the Senator was, how hard it was – impossible, he said, to find the old-fashioned, solid, hard-earned, Uncle Tom type Negra nowadays. I laughed in his face.

GITLOW. Yassuh. By the grace of God, there's still a few of us left.

OL' CAP'N. I told him how you and me growed up together. Had the same mammy – my mammy was your mother.

GITLOW. Yessir! Bosom buddies!

OL' CAP'N. And how you used to sing that favorite ol' speritual of mine:

(Sings.) "I'm a-coming... I'm a-coming, For my head is bending low,"

> *(**GITLOW** joins in on harmony.)*

"I hear the gentle voices calling, Ol' Black Joe..."

> *(This proves too much for **CHARLIE**; he starts out.)*

Where you going?

CHARLIE. Maybe they need me in the front of the store.

OL' CAP'N. Come back here!

> *(**CHARLIE** returns.)*

Turn around – show Gitlow that eye.

> *(**CHARLIE** reluctantly exposes black eye to view.)*

GITLOW. Gret Gawdamighty, somebody done cold cocked this child! Who hit Mr. Charlie, tell Uncle Gitlow who hit you?

> *(**CHARLIE** does not answer.)*

OL' CAP'N. Would you believe it? All of a sudden he can't say a word. And just last night, the boys was telling me, this son of mine made hisself a full-fledged speech.

GITLOW. You don't say.

OL' CAP'N. All about Negras – NeGROES he called 'em – four years of college, and he still can't say the word right – seems he's quite a specialist on the subject.

GITLOW. Well, shut my hard-luck mouth!

OL' CAP'N. Yessireebob. Told the boys over at Ben's bar in town, that he was all for mixing the races together.

GITLOW. You go on 'way from hyeah!

OL' CAP'N. Said white children and darky children ought to go the same schoolhouse together!

GITLOW. Tell me the truth, Ol' Cap'n!

OL' CAP'N. Got hisself so worked up some of 'em had to cool him down with a co-cola bottle!

GITLOW. Tell me the truth – again!

CHARLIE. That wasn't what I said!

OL' CAP'N. You calling me a liar, boy!

CHARLIE. No, sir, but I just said, that since it was the law of the land –

OL' CAP'N. It is not the law of the land no sucha thing!

CHARLIE. I didn't think it would do any harm if they went to school together – that's all.

OL' CAP'N. That's all – that's enough!

CHARLIE. They do it up North –

OL' CAP'N. This is down South. Down here they'll go to school together over me and Gitlow's dead body. Right, Git?!

GITLOW. Er, you the boss, boss!

CHARLIE. But this is the law of the –

OL' CAP'N. Never mind the law! Boy – look! You like Gitlow, you trust him, you always did – didn't you?

CHARLIE. Yessir.

OL' CAP'N. And Gitlow here, would cut off his right arm for you if you was to ask him. Wouldn't you, Git?

GITLOW. *(Gulping.)* You the boss, boss.

OL' CAP'N. Now Gitlow ain't nothing if he ain't a Negra! – Ain't you, Git?

GITLOW. Oh – two-three hundred percent, I calculate.

OL' CAP'N. Now, if you really want to know what the Negra thinks about this here integration and all lacka-that, don't ask the Supreme Court – ask Gitlow. Go ahead – ask him!

CHARLIE. I don't need to ask him.

OL' CAP'N. Then I'll ask him. Raise your right hand, Git. You solemnly swear to tell the truth, whole truth, nothing else but, so help you God?

GITLOW. *(Raising hand.)* I do.

OL' CAP'N. Gitlow Judson, as God is your judge and maker, do you believe in your heart that God intended white folks and Negra children to go to school together?

GITLOW. Nawsuh, I do not!

OL' CAP'N. Do you, so help you God, think that white folks and black should mix and 'sociate in street cars, buses, and railroad stations, in any way, shape, form, or fashion?

GITLOW. Absolutely not!

OL' CAP'N. And is it not your considered opinion, God strike you dead if you lie, that all my Negras are happy with things in the southland just the way they are?

GITLOW. Indeed I do!

OL' CAP'N. Do you think a'ry single darky on my place would ever think of changing a single thing about the South, and to hell with the Supreme Court as God is your judge and maker?

GITLOW. As God is my judge and maker and you are my boss, I do not!

OL' CAP'N. *(Turning in triumph to* **CHARLIE.***)* The voice of the Negra himself! What more proof do you want!

CHARLIE. I don't care whose voice it is – it's still the law of the land, and I intend to obey it!

OL' CAP'N. *(Losing control.)* Get outta my face, boy – get outta my face, before I kill you! Before I –

> (**CHARLIE** *escapes into the commissary.* **OL' CAP'N** *collapses.*)

GITLOW. Easy, Ol' Cap'n, easy, suh, easy!

> (**OL' CAP'N** *gives out a groan.* **GITLOW** *goes to shelf and comes back with a small bottle and a small box.*)

Some aspirins, suh…, some asaphoetida?

> (**PURLIE** *and* **LUTIEBELLE** *appear at door left.*)

Not now – later – later! *(Holds bottle to* **OL' CAP'N***'s nose.)*

OL' CAP'N. Gitlow – Gitlow!

GITLOW. Yassuh, Ol' Cap'n – Gitlow is here, suh; right here!

OL' CAP'N. Quick, ol' friend – my heart. It's – quick! A few passels, if you please – of that ol' speritual.

GITLOW. *(Sings most tenderly.)* "Gone are the days, when my heart was young and gay…"

OL' CAP'N. I can't tell you, Gitlow – how much it eases the pain –

> (**GITLOW** *and* **OL' CAP'N** *sing a phrase together.*)

Why can't he see what they're doing to the southland, Gitlow? Why can't he see it, like you and me? If there's one responsibility you got, boy, above all others, I said to him, it's these Negras – your Negras, boy. Good, honest, hard-working cotton choppers. If you keep after 'em.

GITLOW. Yes, Lawd. *(Continues to sing.)*

OL' CAP'N. Something between you and them no Supreme Court in the world can understand – and wasn't for me they'd starve to death. What's gonna become of 'em, boy, after I'm gone –?

GITLOW. Dass a good question, Lawd – you answer him. *(Continues to sing.)*

OL' CAP'N. They belong to you, boy – to you, evah one of 'em! My ol' Confederate father told me on his deathbed: feed the Negras first – after the horses and cattle – and I've done it evah time!

> *(By now **OL' CAP'N** is sheltered in **GITLOW**'s arms. The lights begin slowly to fade away. **GITLOW** sings a little more.)*

Ah, Gitlow ol' friend – something, absolutely sacred 'bout that speritual – I live for the day you'll sing that thing over my grave.

GITLOW. Me, too, Ol' Cap'n, me, too! *(**GITLOW**'s voice rises to a slow, gentle, yet triumphant crescendo, as our lights fade away.)*

> *(Blackout.)*

Curtain

ACT II

Scene One

(Time: A short while later.)

(Scene: The scene is the same: the little commissary office.)

(At Rise: The stage is empty. After a moment, **GITLOW** *hurries in from the commissary proper, crosses down to the little back door and opens it.)*

PURLIE. *(Entering hurriedly.)* What took you so long?

GITLOW. S-sh! Not so loud! He's right out there in the commissary!

> *(***PURLIE** *crosses over and looks out into the commissary, then crosses back to the little back door and holds out his hands.* **LUTIEBELLE** *enters. She is dressed in what would be collegiate style. She is still full of awe and wonder, and – this time – of fear, which she is struggling to keep under cover.)*

Ain't she gonna carry no school books?

PURLIE. What are they doing out there?

GITLOW. The watermelon books don't balance.

PURLIE. What!

GITLOW. One of our melons is in shortage!

PURLIE. You tell him about Lutiebelle – I mean, about Cousin Bee?

GITLOW. I didn't have time. Besides, I wanted you to have one more chance to get out of here alive!

PURLIE. What's the matter with you?! Don't five hundred dollars of your own lawful money mean nothing to you? Ain't you got no head for business?

GITLOW. No! The head I got is for safekeeping, and – besides –

> (**PURLIE** *lifts Ol' Cap'n's bull whip down from its peg.*)

don't touch that thing, Purlie!

> (**GITLOW** *races over, snatches it from him, replaces it, and pats it soothingly into place, while at the same time looking to see if Ol' Cap'n is coming – and all in one continuous move.*)

PURLIE. Why not? It touched me!

GITLOW. *(Aghast.)* Man, ain't nothing sacred to you?!

OL' CAP'N. *(Calling from off in the commissary.)* Gitlow, come in here!

GITLOW. *(Racing off.)* Coming, Ol' Cap'n, coming!

OL' CAP'N. *(Offstage.)* Now! We are going to cross-examine these watermelons one more time – one watermelon –

GITLOW. *(Offstage.)* One watermelon!

CHARLIE. *(Offstage.)* One watermelon!

OL' CAP'N. *(Offstage.)* Two watermelons –

GITLOW. *(Offstage.)* Two watermelons –

CHARLIE. *(Offstage.)* Two watermelons –

(The sound of the watermelon countdown continues in the background. **PURLIE**, *finding he's got a moment, comes over to reassure* **LUTIEBELLE**.*)*

PURLIE. Whatever you do, don't panic!

LUTIEBELLE. *(Repeating after him: almost in hypnotic rote.)* Whatever you do, don't panic!

PURLIE. Just walk like I taught you to walk, and talk like I taught you to talk –

LUTIEBELLE. Taught like I walked you to –

PURLIE. *(Shaking her shoulders.)* Lutiebelle!

LUTIEBELLE. Yes, Reb'n Purlie!

PURLIE. Wake up!

LUTIEBELLE. Oh my goodness, Reb'n Purlie – was I sleep?

PURLIE. Alert!

LUTIEBELLE. Alert! –

PURLIE. Wide awake! –

LUTIEBELLE. Wide awake! –

PURLIE. Up on your toes!

LUTIEBELLE. *(Starting to rise on toes.)* Up on your –

PURLIE. No. No, that's just a figure of speech. Now! You remember what I told you –?

LUTIEBELLE. No, sir. Can't say I do, sir.

PURLIE. Well – first: chit-chat – small-talk!

LUTIEBELLE. Yessir – how small?

PURLIE. Pass the time of day – you remember? The first thing I taught you on the train?

LUTIEBELLE. On the train – Oh! "Delighted to remake your acquaintance, I am sure."

PURLIE. That's it – that's it exactly! Now. Suppose he was to say to you: *(****PURLIE*** *imitates Ol' Cap'n.)* "I bet you don't remember when you wasn't knee high to a grasshopper and Ol' Cap'n took you by the hand, and led you down on your first trip to the cotton patch?"

LUTIEBELLE. Just like you told me on the train?

PURLIE. Yes!

LUTIEBELLE. "I must confess – that much of my past life is vague and hazy."

PURLIE. *(Imitating.)* Doggone my hide – you're the cutest li'l ol' piece of brown skin sugar I ever did see!

LUTIEBELLE. Oh, thank you, Reb'n Purlie!

PURLIE. I ain't exactly me, saying that – it's Ol' Cap'n. *(Continues imitation.)* And this is my land, and my cotton patch, and my commissary, and my bull whip – still here, just like you left us. And what might be your name, li'l gal?

LUTIEBELLE. *(Warming to the game.)* Beatrice Judson, sir.

PURLIE. And what is your daddy's name, li'l gal?

LUTIEBELLE. Horace Judson, sir.

PURLIE. And what did they teach you up in that college, li'l gal?

LUTIEBELLE. It was my major education, Ol' Cap'n. –

PURLIE. You mean you majored in education. *(Resumes imitation.)* Well – nothing wrong with Negras getting an education, I always say – But then again, ain't nothing right with it, either. Cousin Bee – heh, heh, heh – you don't mind if I call you Cousin Bee, do you, honey?

LUTIEBELLE. Oh, sir, I'd be delighted!

PURLIE. Don't! Don't be delighted until he puts the money in your hands. *(Resumes imitation.)* And where did you say your Maw worked at?

LUTIEBELLE. In North Carolina.

PURLIE. Where is your maw at now?

LUTIEBELLE. She's at the cemetery: she died.

PURLIE. And how much is the inheritance?

LUTIEBELLE. Five hundred dollars for the next of kin.

PURLIE. *(Delighted at her progress.)* Wonderful, just – just – wonderful! *(Enjoying his own imitation now.)*

> *(***OL' CAP'N*** *enters from the commissary, followed by* **GITLOW.** **LUTIEBELLE** *sees* **OL' CAP'N***, but* **PURLIE** *is so wrapped up in his own performance he does not.)*

Say, maybe you could teach a old dog like me some new tricks.

> *(He tries to get a rise out of* **LUTIEBELLE** *but she is frozen in terror.* **OL' CAP'N** *becomes aware of* **PURLIE***'s presence, and approaches.)*

By swickety – a gal like you could doggone well change a joker's luck if she had a mind to – see what I mean?

> *(***PURLIE** *punches what he expects to be an invisible Gitlow in the ribs. His blow lands upon* **OL' CAP'N** *with such force, he falls onto a pile of sacks of chicken feed.)*

OL' CAP'N. *(Sputtering.)* What! What in the name of –

> *(***GITLOW** *and* **PURLIE** *scramble to help him to his feet.)*

PURLIE. My compliments, sir – are only exceeded by my humblest apologies. And allow me, if you please, to present my Aunt Henrietta's daughter, whom you remember so well: Beatrice Judson – or as we call her – Cousin Bee.

OL' CAP'N. *(He is so taken by what he sees, he forgets his anger.)* We'll I'll be switched!

PURLIE. Come, Cousin Bee. Say "howdo" to the man.

LUTIEBELLE. How do to the man. I mean – *(Takes time to correct herself, then.)* Delighted to remake your acquaintance, I'm sure.

OL' CAP'N. What's that? What's that she's saying?

PURLIE. College, sir.

OL' CAP'N. College?

PURLIE. That's all she ever talks.

OL' CAP'N. You mean Henrietta's little ol' button-eyed pickaninny was in college? Well bust my eyes wide open! Just LOOK at that! *(Gets closer, but she edges away.)* You remember me, honey. I'm still the Ol' Cap'n round here.

LUTIEBELLE. Oh, sir, it would not be the same without you being the Ol' Cap'n around here.

OL' CAP'N. You don't say! Say, I'll bet you don't remember a long time ago when –

LUTIEBELLE. When I wasn't but knee high to a hoppergrass, and you took me by the hand, and led me on my very first trip to the cotton patch.

OL' CAP'N. *(Ecstatic.)* You mean you remember that!

LUTIEBELLE. Alert, wide awake, and up on my toes – if you please, sir! *(Rises up on her toes.)*

OL' CAP'N. *(Moving in.)* Doggone my hide. You're the cutest li'l ol' piece of brown sugar I ever did see –

LUTIEBELLE. *(Escaping.)* And this is your land, and your cotton patch, and your commissary, and your bull whip –

OL' CAP'N. What's that?

LUTIEBELLE. Just a figure of speech or two –

OL' CAP'N. Well, Beatrice – you wouldn't mind if Ol' Cap'n was to call you Cousin Bee?

LUTIEBELLE. Oh, positively not, not! – since my mother's name was Henrietta Judson; my father's name was Horace Judson –

OL' CAP'N. But most of all, I remember that little ol' dog of yours – "Spicey," wasn't it?

LUTIEBELLE. Oh, we wasn't much for eating dogs, sir –

OL' CAP'N. No, no! Spicey was the name – wasn't it?

> (**LUTIEBELLE** *looking to* **PURLIE** *for help, but* **PURLIE** *cannot help. He looks to* **GITLOW**, *who also cannot remember.*)

LUTIEBELLE. You, er, really think we really called him "Spicey"?

OL' CAP'N. Not him – her!

PURLIE. HER!

LUTIEBELLE. Oh, her! Her! I am most happy to recollect that I do.

OL' CAP'N. You do! You don't say you do!

LUTIEBELLE. I did, as I recall it, have a fond remembrance of you and "Spicey," since youall went so well together – and at the same time!

OL' CAP'N. You do? Well hush my mouth, eh, Git?

GITLOW. Hush your mouth indeed, sir.

LUTIEBELLE. 'Cose soon it is my sworn and true confession that I disremembers so many things out of my early pastime that mostly you are haze and vaguey!

OL' CAP'N. Oh, am I now!

LUTIEBELLE. Oh, yes, and sir – indeedy.

OL' CAP'N. Doggone my hide, eh, Git?

GITLOW. Doggone your hide indeed, suh.

LUTIEBELLE. You see of coursely I have spount –

PURLIE. Spent –

LUTIEBELLE. Spunt so much of my time among the college that hardly all of my ancient maidenhead –

PURLIE. Hood.

LUTIEBELLE. Is a thing of the past!

OL' CAP'N. You don't say!

LUTIEBELLE. But yes, and most precisely.

OL' CAP'N. Tell me, Li'l Bee – what did they teach you up at that college?

LUTIEBELLE. Well, mostly they taught me an education, but in between I learned a lot, too.

OL' CAP'N. Is that a fact?

LUTIEBELLE. Reading, writing, 'rithmetic – oh, my Lord – just sitting out on the rectangular every evening after four o'clock home work and you have your regular headache –

OL' CAP'N. You know something, I been after these Negras down here for years: Go to school, I'd say, first chance you get – take a coupla courses in advanced cotton picking. But you think they'd listen to me? No sireebob. By swickety! A gal like you could doggone well change a joker's luck if she was a mind to.

> *(Gives* **GITLOW** *a broad wink and digs him in his ribs.* **GITLOW** *almost falls.)*

See what I mean?

LUTIEBELLE. Oh, most indo I deed.

OL' CAP'N. Look – anything! Ask me anything! Whatever you want – name it and it's yours!

LUTIEBELLE. You mean – really, really, really?

OL' CAP'N. Ain't a man in Cotchipee County can beat my time when I see something I want – name it! *(Indicates with a sweep the contents of the commissary.)* Some roasted peanuts; a bottle of soda water; a piece of pep'mint candy?

LUTIEBELLE. Thank you, sir, but if it's all the same to you I'd rather have my money.

OL' CAP'N. *(As if shot.)* Your WHAT!

LUTIEBELLE. *(Frightened but determined to forge ahead under her own steam.)* Now I'm gonna tell you like it was, Your Honor: You see, Reb'n Purlie and Uncle Gitlow had one aunty between them, name of Harrietta –

PURLIE. Henrietta!

LUTIEBELLE. Henrietta – who used to cook for this rich ol' white lady up in North Carolina years ago; and last year this ol' lady died – brain tumor –

PURLIE. Bright's disease!

LUTIEBELLE. Bright's disease – leaving five hundred dollars to every servant who had ever worked on her place, including Henrietta. But Henrietta had already died, herself: largely from smallpox –

PURLIE. No!

LUTIEBELLE. Smally from large pox?

PURLIE. Influenza!

LUTIEBELLE. Influenza – and since Henrietta's husband Harris –

PURLIE. Horace!

LUTIEBELLE. Horace – was already dead from heart trouble –

PURLIE. Gunshot wounds! –

LUTIEBELLE. *(Exploding.)* His heart stopped beating, didn't it?!

PURLIE. Yes, but –

LUTIEBELLE. Precisely, Reb'n Purlie, precisely! *(Turning back to* **OL' CAP'N**.*)* Since, therefore and where-in-as Cousin Bee, her daughter, was first-in-line-for-next-of-kinfolks, the five hundred dollars left in your care and keep by Aunt Henrietta, and which you have been saving just for me all these lonesome years –

OL' CAP'N. I ain't been saving no damn sucha thing!

PURLIE. *(Stepping swiftly into the breach.)* Oh, come out from behind your modesty, sir!

OL' CAP'N. What!

PURLIE. Your kindness, sir; your thoughtfulness, sir; your unflagging consideration for the welfare of your darkies, sir: have rung like the clean clear call of the clarion from Maine to Mexico. Your constant love for them is both hallmark and high water of the true gentility of the dear old South.

OL' CAP'N. Gitlow, Gitlow – go get Charlie. I want him to hear this.

　　　　*(***GITLOW** *exits upstage center.)*

Go on, boy, go on!

PURLIE. And as for your faithful ol' darkies themselves, sir – why, down in the quarters, sir, your name stands second only to God Himself Almighty.

OL' CAP'N. You don't mean to tell me!

PURLIE. Therefore, as a humble token of their high esteem and their deep and abiding affection, especially for saving that five hundred dollar inheritance for Cousin Bee, they have asked me to present to you...this plaque!

*(**PURLIE** unveils a "sheepskin scroll" from his inside coat pocket. **OL' CAP'N** reaches for it, but **PURLIE** draws it away. **CHARLIE** appears in the doorway upstage center followed by **GITLOW**.)*

Which bears the following citation to wit, and I quote: "Whereas Ol' Cap'n has kindly allowed us to remain on his land, and pick his cotton, and tend his cattle, and drive his mules, and whereas Ol' Cap'n still lets us have our hominy grits and fatback on credit and whereas Ol' Cap'n never resorts to bull whip except as a blessing and a benediction, therefore be it resolved, that Ol' Cap'n Cotchipee be cited as the best friend the Negro has ever had, and officially proclaimed Great White Father of the Year!"

OL' CAP'N. *(Stunned.)* I can't believe it – I can't believe it! *(Sees **CHARLIE**.)* Charlie, boy – did you hear it? Did you hear it, Charlie, my boy – GREAT WHITE FATHER OF THE YEAR!

PURLIE. *(Like a professional undertaker.)* Let me be the first to congratulate you, sir.

(They shake hands solemnly.)

OL' CAP'N. Thank you, Purlie.

LUTIEBELLE. And me.

(They shake hands solemnly.)

OL' CAP'N. Thank you, Cousin Bee.

GITLOW. And me, too, Ol' Cap'n.

OL' CAP'N. *(On the verge of tears, as they shake hands.)* Gitlow – Gitlow. I know this is some of your doings – my old friend. *(He turns expectantly to **CHARLIE**.)* Well, boy – *(**CHARLIE** is trapped.)* ain't you gonna congratulate your father?

CHARLIE. Yessir. *(Shakes his hand.)*

OL' CAP'N. This – is the happiest day of my life. My darkies – my Negras – my own – *(Chokes up; unable to continue.)*

PURLIE. Hear, hear!

GITLOW & LUTIEBELLE. Hear, hear!

> *(**CHARLIE** tries to sneak off again, but **OL' CAP'N** sees him.)*

OL' CAP'N. I am just too overcome to talk. Come back here, boy.

> *(**CHARLIE** comes back and stands in intense discomfort.)*

Silent – speechless – dumb, my friends. Never in all the glorious hoary and ancient annals of all Dixie – never before – *(Chokes up with tears; blows nose with big red handkerchief, and pulls himself together.)* My friends, in the holy scripture – and I could cite you chapter and verse if I was a mind to – "In the beginning God created white folks and He created black folks," and in the name of all that's white and holy, let's keep it that way. And to hell with Abraham Lincoln and Martin Luther King!

PURLIE. I am moved, Ol' Cap'n –

GITLOW & LUTIEBELLE. Uhn!

PURLIE. Moved beyond my jurisdiction; as for example, I have upon my person a certificate of legal tender duly affixed and so notarized to said itemized effect – *(Hands over an official-looking document.)* a writ of Habeas Corpus.

OL' CAP'N. *(Taking the document.)* Habeas who?

PURLIE. Habeas Corpus. It means I can have the body.

OL' CAP'N. Body – what body?

PURLIE. The body of the cash – the five hundred dollars – that they sent you to hold in trust for Cousin Bee.

OL' CAP'N. *(Pauses to study the eager faces in the room; then.)* Charlie –

CHARLIE. Yessir.

OL' CAP'N. Bring me – five hundred dollars – will you?

> *(**CHARLIE** starts for safe.)*

No, no, no – not that old stuff. Fresh money, clean money out of my private stock out back. Nothin's too good for my Negras.

CHARLIE. Yessir – yessir! *(Starts out, stops.)* And Paw?

OL' CAP'N. Yes, son?

CHARLIE. All I got to say is "Yessir!" *(Crosses to cash register.)*

OL' CAP'N. Just wait – wait till I tell the Senator: "Great White Father of the Year."

CHARLIE. *(Returns with roll of bills which he hands to his father.)* Here you are, Paw.

OL' CAP'N. Thank you, boy.

> *(Enter **IDELLA**, followed by the **SHERIFF** and the **DEPUTY**.)*

IDELLA. Here everybody is, back in the office.

OL' CAP'N. *(Overjoyed to see them.)* Just in time, Sheriff, for the greatest day of my life. Gentlemen – something has happened here today, between me and my Negras, makes me proud to call myself a Confederate: I have just been named Great White Father of the Year. *(To* **PURLIE**.*)* Right?

PURLIE. Right. And now if you'll just –

SHERIFF & DEPUTY. Great White Father of the Year! Congratulations! *(They shake his hands warmly.)*

OL' CAP'N. True, there are places in this world where the darky is rebellious, running hog wild, rising up and sitting down where he ain't wanted, acting sassy in jail, getting plumb out of hand, totally forgetting his place and his manners – but not in Cotchipee County! *(To* **PURLIE**.*)* Right?

PURLIE. Right! And now perhaps we could get back to the business at hand.

OL' CAP'N. *(Finishing his count.)* All right – five hundred dollars.

> *(***PURLIE** *impulsively reaches for the money, but* **OL' CAP'N** *snatches it back.)*

Just a moment. There's still one small formality: a receipt.

PURLIE. A receipt? All right, I'll –

OL' CAP'N. Not you – You! *(Thrusts a printed form toward* **LUTIEBELLE**.*)* …just for the record. *(Offers her a fountain pen.)* Sign here. Your full and legal name – right here on the dotted line.

PURLIE. *(Reaching for the pen.)* I'll do it – I have her power of attorney.

LUTIEBELLE. *(Beating* **PURLIE** *to the pen.)* It's all right, Reb'n Purlie, I can write. *(Takes pen and signs paper with a flourish.)*

OL' CAP'N. *(Takes up paper and reads the signature.)* Sheriff, I want this woman arrested!

PURLIE. Arrested?! For what?

OL' CAP'N. She came into my presence, together with him – *(Indicates* **PURLIE**.*)* and with him – *(Indicates* **GITLOW**.*)* And they all swore to me that she is Beatrice Judson.

PURLIE. She IS Beatrice Judson!

OL' CAP'N. *(Pouncing.)* Then how come she to sign her name: Lutiebelle Gussiemae Jenkins!

PURLIE. Uhn-uhn!

GITLOW. Uhn-uhn!

LUTIEBELLE. Uhn-uhn!

GITLOW. *(Starting off suddenly.)* Is somebody calling my name out there –

OL' CAP'N. Come back here, Gitlow –

> *(**GITLOW** halts in his tracks.)*

You'll go out of that door when the Sheriff takes you out. And that goes for all of you.

> *(The **SHERIFF** starts forward.)*

Just a minute, Sheriff. Before you take 'em away there's something I've got to do. *(Crosses to where the whip is hung.)*

GITLOW. *(Horrified at the thought of the whip.)* I'll make it up to you in cotton, Ol' Cap'n –

OL' CAP'N. Shut up, Gitlow. *(Takes whip down, and starts to uncoil it.)* Something I started twenty years ago with this bull whip – *(Fastening his eyes on **PURLIE**.)* Something I intend to finish.

GITLOW. *(Drops to his knees and begins to sing.)* "Gone are the days –"

OL' CAP'N. *(Turning to **GITLOW**.)* Dammit! I told you to shut up! *(Then back to **PURLIE**.)* I'm gonna teach you to try to make a damn fool outta white folks; all right, boy, drop them britches.

PURLIE. The hell you preach!

OL' CAP'N. What's that you said?

LUTIEBELLE. He said, "The hell you preach!"

CHARLIE. Paw, wait, listen –!

OL' CAP'N. I thought I told you to shut up! *(Back to* **PURLIE**.*)* Boy, I'm gonna teach you to mind what I say!

> *(***PURLIE** *doesn't move.* **OL' CAP'N** *takes a vicious cut at him with the bull whip, and* **PURLIE***, leaping back to get out of the way, falls into the arms of the* **SHERIFF**.*)*

SHERIFF. I distinctly heard that gentleman order you to drop your britches.

> *(Spins* **PURLIE** *around, sets him up, and swings with all his might.* **PURLIE** *easily ducks and dances away.)*

DEPUTY. Save a little taste for me, Sheriff!

> *(The* **SHERIFF** *swings again; and, again,* **PURLIE** *dances away. He swings still again, but to no avail.)*

SHERIFF. *(Aggravated.)* Hold still, dammit!

> *(Swings again, and once more* **PURLIE** *ducks away.)*

Confound it, boy! You trying to make me hurt myself?

DEPUTY. What's the matter, Sheriff – can't you find him?! *(Laughs.)*

SHERIFF. *(Desperate.)* Now, you listen to me, boy! Either you stand up like a man, so I can knock you down, or –

LUTIEBELLE. *(Stepping between the* **SHERIFF** *and* **PURLIE**.*)* Don't you dare!

SHERIFF. What!

LUTIEBELLE. Insultin' Reb'n Purlie, and him a man of the cloth! *(Grabs his gun arm and bites it.)*

SHERIFF. Owwww! *(She kicks him in the shin.)* Owwwwww!

(The **DEPUTY** *charges in to the rescue. He attempts to grab* **LUTIEBELLE***, but she eludes him and steps down hard on his corns.)*

DEPUTY. Owwwwwwwwww!

PURLIE. *(Going for the* **DEPUTY***.)* Keep your hands off her, you hypothetical baboon, keep your hands OFF her!

(Grabs the **DEPUTY***, spins him around, and knocks him across the room; starts to follow, but the* **SHERIFF** *grabs him and pins his arms behind him.)*

CHARLIE. *(Breaks loose from* **IDELLA***, snatching at the* **SHERIFF***.)* You let him go, dammit, let him go!

(With one arm the **SHERIFF** *pushes* **CHARLIE** *away.)*

SHERIFF. *(Still holding* **PURLIE***'s arms pinned back.)* All right, Dep, he's all yours. Throw him your fast ball – high, tight and inside!

DEPUTY. Glad to oblige you, Sheriff! *(He draws back like a big league baseball pitcher.)*

CHARLIE. *(Rushing into the breach.)* Stop! Stop – stop in the name of the –

(The **DEPUTY** *swings from the floor,* **PURLIE** *ducks and rolls his head sharply to one side.* **CHARLIE** *runs full into the force of the blow. Collapsing heavily.)*

Idella – aaaaaaa!

OL' CAP'N. *(Rushing to him.)* Charlie –!

IDELLA. Charlie –!

*(***PURLIE***, taking advantage of the confusion, snatches* **LUTIEBELLE** *by the arms and dashes with her out the back door.)*

OL' CAP'N. After them, you idiots, after them!

SHERIFF. *(To the* **DEPUTY.***)* After them, you idiot!

> *(They both run off after* **PURLIE** *and* **LUTIEBELLE.**
> **OL' CAP'N** *and* **IDELLA** *are kneeling beside the
> prostrate* **CHARLIE. GITLOW,** *after a moment,
> comes into the picture.)*

OL' CAP'N. His eyes, Idella, his eyes! Where are his eyes?

IDELLA. Gitlow, fetch me the asaphoetida, Ol' Cap'n, you
rub his hands.

GITLOW. Yess'm.

IDELLA. *(Slapping his face.)* Charlie, honey, wake up –
wake up! It's me, Idella.

> *(***OL' CAP'N** *is too disorganized to be of any
> assistance.* **GITLOW** *has returned with a
> bottle which he hands to* **IDELLA.** *He then
> kneels and starts rubbing* **CHARLIE***'s hands.)*

GITLOW. Mr. Charlie, wake up –

> *(With* **GITLOW** *and* **IDELLA***'s help,* **CHARLIE**
> *slowly rises to his feet. Still unsteady, his eyes
> glazed and vacant.)*

OL' CAP'N. *(Snapping his fingers in front of his eyes.)* It's
me, Charlie, me – It's your daddy, boy! Speak to me –
talk to me – say something to me!

CHARLIE. *(Snaps suddenly into speech – but still out on
his feet.)* Fourscore and seven years ago, our fathers
brought forth –

OL' CAP'N. Shut up!

Curtain

Scene Two

(Time: Two days later.)

(Scene: Back at the shack, outside in the yard area.)

*(At Rise: **MISSY** is discovered, busy working on some potted plants. She is preoccupied, but we feel some restlessness, some anticipation in the manner in which she works. **PURLIE** enters.)*

PURLIE. *(The great prophet intones his sorrows.)* Toll the bell – Big Bethel; toll the big, black, ex-liberty bell; tell Freedom there's death in the family.

MISSY. Purlie –

PURLIE. All these wings and they still won't let me fly!

MISSY. Where you been these last two days, Purlie? We been lookin' for you. All this plotting and planning – risking your dad-blasted neck like a crazy man! And for what – FOR WHAT!

*(**IDELLA** enters.)*

Oh, come in, Miz Idella.

IDELLA. Is anybody here seen Charlie Cotchipee this morning?

MISSY. No, we haven't.

PURLIE. Is something wrong, Miz Idella?

IDELLA. He left home this morning right after breakfast – here it is after lunch and I ain't seen him since. I can't find Charlie – first time in forty-five years I been working up there in that house I ever misplaced anything! You don't suppose he'd run away from home and not take me –?

MISSY. Oh, no, Miz Idella! Not li'l Charlie Cotchipee.

IDELLA. Well, I guess I'd better be getting back. If you should see him –

MISSY. Miz Idella, we all want to thank you for keeping Purlie out of jail so kindly. *(Hands her flowers.)*

IDELLA. Oh, that was nothing; I just told that ol' man if he didn't stop all that foolishness about chain gangs and stuff, I would resign from his kitchen and take Charlie right along with me! But now I've lost Charlie. First time in forty-five years I ever misplaced anything! *(She exits.)*

MISSY. *(Turns to* **PURLIE**.*)* Don't you know there's something more important in this world than having that broken down ol' ex-church of a barn to preach in?

PURLIE. Yeah – like what?

MISSY. Like asking Lutiebelle to marry you.

PURLIE. Asking Lutiebelle to marry me?

MISSY. She worships the ground you walk on. Talks about you all the time. You two could get married, settle down, like you ought to, and raise the cutest little ol' family you ever did see. And she's a cookin', po' child – she left you some of her special fritters.

PURLIE. Freedom, Missy, not fritters. The crying need of this Negro day and age is not grits, but greatness; not cornbread but courage; not fat-back, but fight-back; Big Bethel is my Bethel; it belongs to me and to my people; and I intend to have it back if I have to pay for it in blood!

MISSY. All right – come on in and I'll fix you some dinner.

GITLOW. *(Enters front door, singing.)* "I'm comin', I'm comin' –"

MISSY. *(Entering house.)* Not so loud, Gitlow. You want to wake up the mule?

GITLOW. Not on his day off. "For my head is bendin' low –" *(**GITLOW** sits, unfolds comic section and reads.)*

MISSY. Where's Lutiebelle, Gitlow?

GITLOW. "The history of the War Between the States will be continued next week." That sure is a good story – I wonder how that's gonna come out?

MISSY. Grown man, deacon in the church, reading the funny-paper. And your shirt. You sneaked outta here this morning in your clean white shirt, after I told you time and time again I was saving it!

GITLOW. Saving it for what?

MISSY. It's the only decent thing you got to get buried in! *(Exits side door.)*

GITLOW. Don't you know that arrangements for my funeral has been taken over by the white folks? *(To **PURLIE**.)* Besides, I got the money!

PURLIE. What kinda money?

GITLOW. The five hundred dollar kinda money.

PURLIE. Five hundred dollars! You mean Ol' Cap'n give the money to you?

GITLOW. "Gitlow," he said. "Ain't another man in this valley, black, white, or otherwise, I would trust to defend and protect me from the N double ACP but you."

PURLIE. Is that a fact?

GITLOW. Well, now. Whatever become of you? All them gretgawdamighty plans your mouth runneth over – all that white folks' psychology?

PURLIE. Gitlow! Er, Deacon Gitlow – Big Bethel is waiting!

GITLOW. So you're the good-for-nothing, raggedy ass high falute 'round here that goes for who-tied-the-bear!

PURLIE. Naw, Git, man – ain't nothing to me.

GITLOW. Always so high and mighty – can't nobody on earth handle white folks but you – don't pay no 'tention to Gitlow; naw – he's a Tom. Tease him – low-rate him – laugh at ol' Gitlow; he ain't nothing but a fool!

PURLIE. Aw, Git, man, you got me wrong. I didn't mean nothing like that!

GITLOW. Who's the fool now, my boy – who's the fool now?

PURLIE. Er – I'm the fool, Gitlow.

GITLOW. Aw, man, you can talk plainer than that.

PURLIE. I'm the fool, Gitlow.

GITLOW. Uh-huh! Now go over to that window, open it wide as it will go and say it so everybody in this whole damn valley can hear you! Go on! Go on, man – I ain't got all day!

PURLIE. *(Goes to window.)* I'm the fool, Gitlow!

GITLOW. Nice. Now beg me!

PURLIE. What!

GITLOW. I said if you want to see the money, beg me! Do it like you do white folks.

PURLIE. I'd rather die and go to hell in a pair gasoline drawers –

   *(**GITLOW** starts to put money away.)*

No, wait. Holy mackerel, dere, Massa Gitlow – hee, hee, hee. Hey! Boss, could I possible have a look at that there five hundred dollars dere, suh? Hyuh, hyuh, hyuh!

GITLOW. Man, you sure got style! You know together you and me could make the big time!

   *(**PURLIE** reaches for money.)*

Come in and see me during office hours! As Deputy-For-The-Colored, I guess I'll just sort of step outside for a minute and let that low September sun shine down on a joker as rich as he is black!

PURLIE. Gitlow – Gitlow!

(**GITLOW** *starts for side door.*)

If slavery ever comes back I want to be your agent!

GITLOW. Now that was a snaggy-toothed, poverty-struck remark if I ever heard one.

MISSY. *(Enters side door.)* Youall wash your hands and git ready – Gitlow! Where's Lutiebelle?

GITLOW. *(Evasive.)* She didn't get back yet.

MISSY. We know she didn't get back yet.

PURLIE. Where is Lutiebelle, Gitlow?

GITLOW. What I mean is – on our way home from church, we stopped by Ol' Cap'n's awhile, and he asked me to leave her there to help with the Sunday dinner.

PURLIE. And you left her!

MISSY. With that frisky ol' man?

GITLOW. For goodness' sakes, she's only waiting on table.

PURLIE. The woman I love don't wait on table for nobody, especially Ol' Cap'n; I know that scoun'. I'm going and get her!

GITLOW. Wait a minute – you can't get her right now!

PURLIE. *(Studying him.)* What you mean, I can't get her right now?

GITLOW. Not right this minute – that'll spoil everything. Ol' Cap'n wouldn't like it.

MISSY. How low can you git, Gitlow!

GITLOW. I mean she's got to stay and bring us the five hundred dollars.

MISSY. What five hundred dollars?

PURLIE. I thought you already had the money?

GITLOW. Well, not exactly. But he promised me faithful to send it down by Lutiebelle.

PURLIE. I'm going and get Lutiebelle –

GITLOW. Wait a minute, wait a minute; you want to buy Big Bethel back or don't you?

PURLIE. *(A glimmering of truth.)* I hope I misunderstand you!

GITLOW. You said it yourself: It is meet that the daughters of Zion should sacrifice themselves for the cause.

PURLIE. *(Grabbing up Missy's bat.)* Gitlow, I'll kill you –!

GITLOW. Wait a minute, wait a minute, wait a MINUTE!

> *(The door opens suddenly, and there stands* **LUTIEBELLE**. *She, too, has on her Sunday best, but it is disheveled. She has a work apron over her dress, with her hat completely askew, the once proud feather now hanging over her face. In her hands she still clutches a rolling pin.)*

MISSY. Lutiebelle – Lutiebelle, honey!

LUTIEBELLE. I think I am going to faint.

> *(She starts to collapse, and they rush toward her to help; but suddenly she straightens up and waves them off.)*

No, I ain't, either – I'm too mad! *(She shudders in recollection.)* I was never so insulted in all my dad-blamed life!

PURLIE. Lutiebelle!

LUTIEBELLE. Oh, excuse me, Reb'n Purlie – I know I look a mess, but –

MISSY. What happened up there?

LUTIEBELLE. *(Boiling again.)* I'm a maid first class, Aunt Missy, and I'm proud of it!

MISSY. Of course you are.

LUTIEBELLE. I ain't had no complaints to speak of since first I stepped into the white folks' kitchen. I'm clean; I'm honest, and I work hard – but one thing: I don't stand for no stuff from them white folks.

PURLIE. Of course you don't. You don't have to –

LUTIEBELLE. I mean, I KNOW my job, and I DO my job – and the next ol' sweaty, ol' grimey, ol' drunkeny man puts his hands on me – so much as touch like he got no business doing – God grant me strength to kill him! Excuse me, Reb'n Purlie.

GITLOW. Well, Ol' Cap'n do get playful at times – did he send the money?

LUTIEBELLE. Money! What money? There ain't none!

GITLOW. What! Naw, naw! He wouldn't do that to me – not to good ol', faithful ol' Gitlow, nawsir!

LUTIEBELLE. The whole thing was a trick – to get you out of the house –

GITLOW. Not to ME he didn't!

LUTIEBELLE. So he could – sneak up behind me in the pantry!

MISSY. What I tell you! – what I tell you!

LUTIEBELLE. I knowed the minute I – Come grabbing on me, Reb'n Purlie; come grabbing his dirty ol' hands on me!

PURLIE. He did!

LUTIEBELLE. And twisting me around, and – and pinching me, Reb'n Purlie!

PURLIE. Pinching you – where? Where?

LUTIEBELLE. Must I, Reb'n Purlie –?

PURLIE. I demand to know – where did he pinch you!

> (**LUTIEBELLE** *diffidently locates a spot on her left cheek. They all examine it anxiously.*)

MISSY. That's him all right!

GITLOW. Aw, Missy –

MISSY. I'd know them fingerprints anywhere!

LUTIEBELLE. Right in the pantry – and then he, he – Oh, Reb'n Purlie, I'm so ashamed!

PURLIE. What did he do? Tell me, woman, tell me: what did he do? WHAT DID HE DO?

LUTIEBELLE. He kissed me!

PURLIE & MISSY. No!

LUTIEBELLE. He kissed me – right here.

MISSY. *(Squinting, it is a very small spot indeed.)* Right where?

> (**LUTIEBELLE** *is so broken up, she can only point to her other cheek.*)

GITLOW. Aw, for Pete's sakes.

PURLIE. *(Almost out of control.)* He kissed my woman, Gitlow – he kissed the woman I love!

GITLOW. So what!

PURLIE. So what do you mean, "So what"? No man kisses the woman I love and lives!

> (**GITLOW** *laughs.*)

Go ahead, laugh! Laugh. Let's have one last look at your teeth before I knock 'em down your throat!

GITLOW. Aw, man, git off my nerves.

PURLIE. I'm going up that hill, and I'm gonna call that buzzardly ol' bastard out, and I wouldn't be surprised if I didn't beat him until he died.

LUTIEBELLE. *(Suddenly not so sure.)* Reb'n Purlie –

GITLOW. *(Also wondering about **PURLIE**.)* Now looka here, Purlie – don't you be no fool, boy – you still in Georgia. If you just got to defend the honor of the woman you love, do it somewhere else.

PURLIE. Kissing my woman – kissing my woman! *(Runs to window, flings it open and shouts out.)* Man, I'll break your neck off!

>   *(**LUTIEBELLE** helps **GITLOW** and **MISSY** to wrestle **PURLIE** away from the window.)*

LUTIEBELLE. Please, Reb'n Purlie!

PURLIE. *(Breaks away and goes to window and shouts again.)* I'll stomp your eyeballs in!

>   *(They snatch him from the window again.)*

LUTIEBELLE. Don't, Reb'n Purlie – oh my goodness! –

PURLIE. *(Breaks away still again and shouts from window.)* I'll snatch your right arm outta the socket, and beat the rest of you to death!

>   *(This time they get him away, and close the window.)*

LUTIEBELLE. Don't talk like that, Reb'n Purlie!

MISSY. *(Standing at the window, arms widespread to block him.)* Have you gone crazy?

GITLOW. *(Still struggling with **PURLIE**.)* You go up that hill tonight, boy, and they'll kill you!

PURLIE. Let 'em kill me, it won't be the first time.

LUTIEBELLE. Aunt Missy, stop him –

GITLOW. Listen, boy! This is your Deputy-For-The-Colored telling you you ain't gonna leave this house, and that's an order!

PURLIE. You try and stop me!

GITLOW. Good gracious a life, what's the matter with you? The man only kissed your woman.

PURLIE. Yeah! And what you suppose he'd a done to me if I'd a kissed his? *(The one question too obvious to answer.)* And that's exactly what I'm gonna do to him!

LUTIEBELLE. Please, Reb'n Purlie. I beg you on bended knees. *(She throws her arms around him.)*

PURLIE. *(Holds her close.)* For the glory and honor of the Negro National Anthem; for the glory and honor of brown-skin Negro womanhood; for the glory and honor of –

> *(***LUTIEBELLE*** *suddenly kisses him big and hard.)*

– for LUTIEBELLE! *(His emotions explode him out of the door which slams shut behind him.)*

GITLOW. *(Singing.)* "I hear them gentle bloodhounds callin' – Old Black Joe..."

> *(***LUTIEBELLE*** *finds the deepest spot in* ***MISSY****'s shoulder to bury her head and cry, as:)*

Curtain

ACT III

Scene One

(Time: Later that same night.)

(Scene: The shack.)

(At Rise: There is light only from a kerosene lamp turned down low. The air of Sunday is gone from the room. The tablecloth has been changed, and things are as they were before. **LUTIEBELLE** *enters down right.)*

LUTIEBELLE. Is it him, Aunt Missy, is it him?

MISSY. No, honey, not yet.

LUTIEBELLE. Oh, I could have sworn I thought it was him. What time is it?

MISSY. About four in the morning from the sound of the birds. Now, why ain't you sleep after all that hot toddy I give you?

LUTIEBELLE. I can't sleep. The strangest thing. I keep hearing bells –

MISSY. Bells?

LUTIEBELLE. Wedding bells. Ain't that funny? Oh, Lord, please don't let him be hurt bad, please! Where can he be, Aunt Missy?

MISSY. Now don't you worry 'bout Purlie. My! You put on your pretty pink dress!

LUTIEBELLE. Yes, ma'am. It's the only thing I got fitting to propose in.

MISSY. Oh?

LUTIEBELLE. I thought, to sort of show my gratitude, I'd offer him my hand in matrimony – it's all I've got.

MISSY. It's a nice hand, and a nice dress – just right for matrimony.

LUTIEBELLE. You really think so, Aunt Missy: really, really, really?

MISSY. I know so, and wherever Reb'n Purlie is this morning, you can bet your bottom dollar he knows it, too.

LUTIEBELLE. Ten thousand Queens of Sheba! Aunt Missy –

MISSY. Yes –

LUTIEBELLE. *(Letting it out in a gush.)* I wanted him to get mad; I wanted him to tear out up that hill; I wanted him to punch that sweaty ol' buzzard in his gizzard – You think I was wrong?

MISSY. I should say not!

LUTIEBELLE. Course I coulda punched him myself, I reckon.

MISSY. Why should you? Why shouldn't our men folks defend our honor with the white folks once in a while? They ain't got nothing else to do.

LUTIEBELLE. You really, really, really think so?

MISSY. *(Shrugs.)* Ten thousand Queens of Sheba –

LUTIEBELLE. Oh, my goodness, when he walks through that door, I'm just gonna –

> *(Door down left suddenly swings open to reveal **GITLOW**.)*

GITLOW. *(Entering.)* Well, well, Lutiebelle.

LUTIEBELLE. Did you find him, Uncle Git?

MISSY. Don't depend on Gitlow for nothing, honey – *(Exits to kitchen.)*

LUTIEBELLE. Where can he be, Uncle Gitlow, where can he be?

GITLOW. Oh – good wind like this on his tail oughta put him somewhere above Macon long 'bout now, if his shoes hold out!

LUTIEBELLE. You mean – running!

GITLOW. What's wrong with running? It emancipated more people than Abe Lincoln ever did.

LUTIEBELLE. How dare you! The finest, bravest man –

GITLOW. The finer they come, the braver they be, the deader these white folks gonna kill 'em when they catch 'em!

MISSY. *(Entering from the kitchen.)* Gitlow, I'll skin you!

GITLOW. All that talk about calling that man out, and whipping him –

MISSY. A man is duty-bound to defend the honor of the woman he loves, and any woman worth her salt will tell you so.

LUTIEBELLE. Love can make you do things you really can't do – can't it, Aunt Missy?

GITLOW. Look. That man's got the president, the governor, the courthouse, and both houses of the congress – on his side!

MISSY. Purlie Judson is a man the Negro woman can depend on!

LUTIEBELLE. An honor to his race, and a credit to his people!

GITLOW. *(Not to be sidetracked.)* The army, the navy, the marines; the Sheriff, the judge, the jury, the police, the F.B.I. – all on his side. Not to mention a pair of brass knucks and the hungriest dogs this side of hell! Surely youall don't expect that po' boy to go up against all that caucasiatic power empty-handed!

MISSY. O, ye of little faith!

LUTIEBELLE. Didn't my Lord deliver Daniel?

GITLOW. Of course he did – but lions is one thing and white folks is another!

MISSY. Where there's a will there's a woman –

LUTIEBELLE. And where there's a woman there's a way!

GITLOW. *(Exasperated.)* Great Gawdamighty! All right – go ahead and have it your way. But I'll lay you six bits 'gainst half my seat on the heavenly choir, Purlie ain't been up that hill. And the minute he walks in that door – if he ever shows up again around here – I'm gonna prove it! Oh, damn – I can make better time out there talkin' to that mule.

MISSY. Why not – it's one jackass to another.

> *(**GITLOW** exits to the kitchen. **MISSY** and **LUTIEBELLE** look at each other, both determined not to give way to the very real fright they feel. There is a long, uncomfortable pause.)*

LUTIEBELLE. It sure is a lovely year – for this time of morning, I mean. *(There is a pause.)* I can't tell you how much all this fresh-air, wine-smoke, and apple-bite reminds me of Alabama.

MISSY. Oh, yes – Ol' Georgia can sure smile pretty when she's of a mind to –

PURLIE. *(Bursts in.)* "Arise and shine for thy light has come."

MISSY. Purlie – Purlie Victorious! *(They embrace.)*

LUTIEBELLE. Oh, you Reb'n Purlie you!

PURLIE. "Truth and Mercy are met together, Righteousness and Peace have kissed each other!" *(They embrace.)*

MISSY. Let me look at you – behold the man! – knee-deep in shining glory. Great day the righteous marching! What happened to you?

PURLIE. Mine enemy hath been destroyed!

MISSY. What!

PURLIE. I told that ol' man twenty years ago, Missy, that over his dead body, Big Bethel would rise again!

MISSY. Purlie –! You mean you done –

PURLIE. "Have I any pleasure that the wicked should die, saith the Lord, and not turn from his ways and live?" Lutiebelle, put on your hat and coat, and hurry!

LUTIEBELLE. Yessir!

PURLIE. Missy, throw us some breakfast into a paper sack, and quick!

MISSY. Yessir!

PURLIE. Gitlow, I'm calling on you and your fellow mule to write a new page in the annals of Negro History Week.

GITLOW. *(Entering.)* Well, if it ain't ol' little black riding hood, dere! How was the mean ol' peckerwolf tonight, dere, kingfish?

MISSY. Tell him, Purlie boy, what you told us: how you sashayed up that hill with force and fistfight!

GITLOW. Hallelujah!

MISSY. How you fit Ol' Cap'n to a halt and a standstill!

GITLOW. Talk that talk!

MISSY. And left him laying in a pool of his own Confederate blood!

GITLOW. For Pete sakes, Missy – quit lying!

MISSY. Don't you dare call Purlie Judson a liar!

LUTIEBELLE. No man calls Reb'n Purlie a liar and lives!

GITLOW. What's the matter with you people? Purlie ain't been up that hill; Purlie ain't seen Ol' Cap'n; Purlie ain't done doodley squat! And all that gabble about leaving somebody in a pool of his own Confederate blood ain't what the bull left in the barnyard!

PURLIE. Five hundred dollars says it is! *(Draws roll of bills from his pocket, for all to see.)*

ALL. Five hundred dollars!

PURLIE. In cool September cash!

GITLOW. Money!

> *(Lunges forward, but **PURLIE** slaps his hand.)*

PURLIE. And that ain't all I got – *(Opens bag he has brought. They look in.)*

GITLOW. *(Almost choking in awe.)* Oh, my goodness, Missy – great day in the morning time – Missy – Missy!

MISSY. *(Also impressed.)* Gitlow, that's *it*!

GITLOW. That's *it*, Missy – that's *it*!

MISSY. Of course that's *it*! – ain't nothing in the world but *it*!

> *(**PURLIE** slowly pulls out Ol' Cap'n's bull whip.)*

GITLOW. Ain't but one way – one way in all this world – for nobody to get that bull whip off'n Ol' Cap'n!

MISSY. And that's off'n his dead body!

GITLOW. And that's the everlovin' truth, so help me.

PURLIE. Here, take it – and burn it in a public place. Lutiebelle –

LUTIEBELLE. Yes, Reb'n Purlie.

PURLIE. This money belongs to the Negro people –

GITLOW. Reb'n Purlie, my boy, I apologize from the bottom of my knees. *(Kneels and starts to sing.)* "Gone are the days –"

MISSY. *(Snatching him to his feet.)* Get up and shut up!

PURLIE. *(Deliberately continuing to **LUTIEBELLE**.)* Take it, and wear it next to your heart.

LUTIEBELLE. *(Very conscious of the great charge laid upon her, turns her back to **GITLOW** and hides the money in her bosom.)* Until death us do part.

MISSY. *(To **GITLOW**.)* If I ever catch you with that song in your mouth again I'll choke you with it!

PURLIE. And go wake up the mule. We due in Waycross to buy Big Bethel.

GITLOW. I'm going, I'm going. *(Starts, but can't tear himself away.)* Cash – five hundred dollars in cash. And a bull whip, from Ol' Cap'n Cotchipee himself – Man, I'd give a pretty piece of puddin' to know how you did it!

MISSY. You go and wake up that mule! *(Turning back to **PURLIE**.)* Me, too! How did you do it, Purlie?

LUTIEBELLE. What happened when you first got there?

PURLIE. *(Almost laughing.)* Now wait a minute – don't rush me!

MISSY. That's what I say: don't rush him – let the man talk!

PURLIE. Talk! Missy, I told you. I haven't got time –

GITLOW. That's all right, Purlie, we'll listen in a hurry.

LUTIEBELLE. What happened when you called him out and whipped him?

PURLIE. I didn't call him out and whip him!

GITLOW. What!

MISSY. You didn't!

LUTIEBELLE. Reb'n Purlie –?

PURLIE. I mean, I did call him out –!

LUTIEBELLE. *(In ecstatic relief.)* Oh – You did call him out!

PURLIE. Yeah – but he didn't come.

ALL. What!

PURLIE. So – er – I went in to get him!

ALL. You did! Sure enough! What happened then?

PURLIE. *(Still seeking escape.)* Well, like I told you –

LUTIEBELLE. Tell us, Reb'n Purlie – please!

PURLIE. *(No escape.)* Well – here was me; and there was him – twisted and bent like a pretzel! Face twitchified like a pan of worms; eyes bugging out; sweat dreening down like rain; tongue plumb clove to the roof of his mouth! *(He looks to his audience, and is impelled to go on.)* Well – this thief! This murderer; this adulterer – this oppressor of all my people, just a sitting there: Stonewall Jackson Cotchipee, just a sitting there. *(Begins to respond to his own fantasy.)* "Go to, rich man, weep and howl, for your sorrows shall come upon you." And-a "Wherefore abhor yourself, and repent Ye in sackcloth and ashes!" 'cause ol' Purlie is done come to get you!

LUTIEBELLE. *(Swept away.)* Oh, my Lord!

MISSY. What he do, Purlie – what he do?!

PURLIE. Fell down on bended knees and cried like a baby!

MISSY. Ol' Cap'n Cotchipee on his knees?!

GITLOW. Great day in the morning time!

PURLIE. *(Warming to the task.)* Don't beg me, white folks, it's too late. "Mercy?" What do you know about mercy?! Did you have mercy on Ol' Uncle Tubb when he asked you not to cheat him out of his money so hard, and you knocked him deaf in his left ear? – Did you have mercy on Lolly's boy when he sassed you back, and you took and dipped his head in a bucket of syrup! And twenty years ago when little Purlie, black and manly as he could be, stood naked before you and your bull whip and pleaded with tears in his li'l ol' eyes, did you have mercy?!

GITLOW. Naw!

PURLIE. – And I'll not have mercy now!

ALL. Amen! Help him, Lawd! Preach it, boy, preach it! *(Etc.)*

PURLIE. Vengeance is mine saith the Lord! *(Hallelujah!)* Ye serpents; ye vipers; ye low-down sons of –! *(Amen!)* How can ye escape the damnation of hell!

MISSY. Throw it at him, boy!

PURLIE. And then, bless my soul, I looked up – up from the blazing depths of my righteous indignation! And I saw tears spill over from his eyeballs; and I heard the heart be-clutching anguish of his outcry! His hands was both a-tremble; and slobber a-dribblin' down his lips!

GITLOW. Oh, my Lawd!

PURLIE. And he whined and whimpered like a ol' hound dog don't want you to kick him no more!

LUTIEBELLE. Great goodness a mighty!

PURLIE. And I commenced to ponder the meaning of this evil thing that groveled beneath my footstool – this no-good lump of nobody! – not fit to dwell on this earth beside the children of the blessed – an abomination to the Almighty and stench in the nostrils of his people! And yet – *(Pause for effect.)* And yet – a man! A weak man; a scared man; a pitiful man; like the whole southland bogged down in sin and segregation crawling on his knees before my judgment seat – but still a MAN!

GITLOW. A man, Lawd!

PURLIE. He, too, like all the South, was one of God's creatures –

MISSY. Yes, Lawd!

PURLIE. He, too, like all the South, could never be beyond the reach of love, hope, and redemption.

LUTIEBELLE. Amen!

PURLIE. Somewhere for him – even for him, some father's heart was broken, some mother's tears undried.

GITLOW. Dry 'em, Lawd!

PURLIE. I am my brother's keeper!

ALL. Yes, Lawd.

PURLIE. And thinking on these things, I found myself to pause, and stumble in my great resolve – and sorrow squeezed all fury from my heart – and pity plucked all hatred from my soul – and the racing feet of an avenging anger slowed down to a halt and a standstill – and the big, black, and burly fist of my strong correction – raised on high like a stroke of God's own lightning – fell useless by my side. The book say, "Love one another."

MISSY. Love one another!

PURLIE. The book say, "Comfort ye one another."

LUTIEBELLE. Comfort ye one another.

PURLIE. The book say, "Forgive ye one another."

GITLOW. Forgive Ol' Cap'n, Lord.

PURLIE. Slowly I turned away – to leave this lump of human mess and misery to the infinite darkness of a hell for white folks only, when suddenly –

MISSY. Suddenly, Lord.

PURLIE. Suddenly I put on my brakes – Purlie Victorious Judson stopped dead in his tracks – and stood stark still, and planted his feet, and rared back, asked himself and all the powers – that – be some mighty important questions.

LUTIEBELLE. Yes, he did, Lawd.

MISSY. And that is the truth!

PURLIE. How come – I asked myself, it's always the colored folks got to do all the forgiving?

GITLOW. Man, you mighty right!

PURLIE. How come the only cheek gits turned in this country is the Negro cheek!

MISSY. Preach to me, boy!

PURLIE. What was this, this – man – Ol' Cap'n Cotchipee – that in spite of all his sins and evils, he still had dominion over me?

LUTIEBELLE. Ain't that the truth!

PURLIE. God made us all equal – God made us all brothers –

ALL. Amen, amen.

PURLIE. "And hath made of one blood all nations of men for to dwell on the face of the earth." – Who changed all that?!

GITLOW. *(Furious.)* Who changed it, he said.

PURLIE. Who took it and twisted it around!

MISSY. *(Furious.)* Who was it, he said!

LUTIEBELLE. *(Furious.)* And where's that scoun' hiding?!

PURLIE. So that the Declarator of Independence himself might seem to be a liar?

GITLOW. Who, that's what I want to know, who?

PURLIE. That a man the color of his face – *(Pointing up Cotchipee Hill.)* could live by the sweat of a man the color of mine!

LUTIEBELLE. Work with him, Lawd, work with him!

PURLIE. – Could live away up there in his fine, white mansion, and us down here in a shack not fitting to house the fleas upon his dogs!

GITLOW. Nothing but fleas!

PURLIE. – Could wax hisself fat on the fat of the land; steaks, rice, chicken, roastineers, sweet potato pies, hot buttered biscuits and cane syrup anytime he felt like it and never hit a lick at a snake! And us got to every day git-up-and-git-with-it, sunup-to-sundown, on fat-back and cornmeal hoecakes – and don't wind up owning enough ground to get buried standing up in!

MISSY. Do, Lord!

PURLIE. – And horses and cadillacs, bull whips and bourbon, and two for 'leven dollar seegars – and our fine young men to serve at his table; and our fine young women to serve in his bed!

LUTIEBELLE. Help him, Lawd.

PURLIE. Who made it like this – who put the white man on top?

GITLOW. That's what I wants to know!

PURLIE. Surely not the Lord God of Israel who is a just God!

MISSY. Hah, Lord!

PURLIE. And no respecter of persons! Who proved in the American Revolution that all men are created equal!

GITLOW. Man, I was there when he proved it!

PURLIE. Endowed with Civil Rights and First Class Citizenship, Ku Klux Klan, White Citizens Council notwithstanding!

MISSY. Oh, yes, he did!

PURLIE. And when my mind commenced to commemorate and to reconsider all these things –

GITLOW. Watch him, Lawd!

PURLIE. And I thought of the black mother in bondage – *(Yes.)* and I thought of the black father in prison – *(Ha, Lawd!)* And of Momma herself – Missy can tell how pretty she was –

MISSY. Indeed I can!

PURLIE. How she died outdoors on a dirty sheet 'cause the hospital doors said – "For white folks only." And of Papa, God rest his soul – who brought her tender loving body back home – and laid her to sleep in the graveyard – and cried himself to death among his children!

MISSY. *(Crying.)* Purlie, Purlie –

PURLIE. *(Really carried away.)* Then did the wrath of a righteous God possess me; and the strength of the host and of ten thousand swept into my good right arm – and I arose and I smote Ol' Cap'n a mighty blow! And the wind from my fist ripped the curtains from the eastern walls – and I felt the weight of his ol' bull whip nestling in my hands – and the fury of a good Gawd-almighty was within me; and I beat him – I whipped him – and I flogged him – and I cut him – I destroyed him!

> *(**IDELLA** enters.)*

GITLOW. Great day and the righteous marching – Whoeeeee! Man, I ain't been stirred that deep since the tree caught fire on a possum hunt and the dogs pushed Papa in the pot.

MISSY. Idella, you shoulda heard him!

IDELLA. I did hear him – all the way across the valley. I thought he was calling hogs. Well, anyway: all hell is broke loose at the big house. Purlie, you better get outta here. Ol' Cap'n is on the phone to the Sheriff.

MISSY. Ol' Cap'n Cotchipee is dead.

IDELLA. The hell you preach.

ALL. What!

IDELLA. Ol' Cap'n ain't no more dead than I am.

LUTIEBELLE. That's a mighty tacky thing to say about your ex-fellow man.

MISSY. Mighty tacky.

LUTIEBELLE. Reb'n Purlie just got through preaching 'bout it. How he marched up Cotchipee hill –

GITLOW. *(Showing the bull whip.)* And took Ol' Cap'n by the bull whip –

MISSY. And beat that ol' buzzard to death!

IDELLA. That is the biggest lie since the devil learned to talk!

LUTIEBELLE. I am not leaving this room till somebody apologizes to Reb'n Purlie V. Judson, the gentleman of my intended.

IDELLA. Purlie Judson! Are you gonna stand there sitting on your behind, and preach these people into believing you spent the night up at the big house whipping Ol' Cap'n to death when all the time you was breaking into the commissary!

MISSY. Breaking into the commissary!

GITLOW. Something is rotten in the cotton!

PURLIE. It's all right, Miz Idella – I'll take it from there –

MISSY. It is not all right –!

PURLIE. While it is true that, maybe, I did not go up that hill just word for word, and call that ol' man out, and beat him to death so much on the dotted line –!

MISSY. *(Snatching up the paper bag.)* I'm goin' to take back my lunch!

PURLIE. Missy! Wait a minute!

LUTIEBELLE. You know what, Aunt Missy?

MISSY. Yes, honey?

LUTIEBELLE. Sometimes I just wish I could drop dead for a while!

PURLIE. Wait, Lutiebelle, give me a chance to –

LUTIEBELLE. Here's your money! – *(Puts roll into* **PURLIE***'s hand.)* And that goes for every other great big ol' handsome man in the whole world!

PURLIE. What you want me to do? Go up that hill by myself and get my brains knocked out?

MISSY. It's little enough for the woman you love!

LUTIEBELLE. Why'd you have to preach all them wonderful things that wasn't so?

GITLOW. And why'd you have to go and change your mind?

PURLIE. I didn't mean for them not to be so: it was a – a parable! A prophecy! Believe me! I ain't never in all my life told a lie I didn't mean to make come true, some day! Lutiebelle –!

IDELLA. Purlie: unless you want to give heartbreak a headache, you better run!

PURLIE. Run – run for what!

MISSY. You want Ol' Cap'n to catch you here?!

PURLIE. Confound Ol' Cap'n! Dad-blast Ol' Cap'n! Damn, damn, damn, and double-damn Ol' Cap'n!

> *(The front door swings open and in walks* **OL' CAP'N** *steaming with anger.)*

OL' CAP'N. *(Controlling himself with great difficulty.)* Somebody – I say somebody – is calling my name!

GITLOW. Ol' Cap'n, you just in time to settle a argument: is Rudolph Valentino still dead?

OL' CAP'N. Shut up!

GITLOW. *(To* **MISSY***.)* See – I told you.

OL' CAP'N. One thing I have not allowed in my cotton patch since am-I-born-to-die! And that's stealin'! Somebody broke into my commissary tonight – took two cans of sardines, a box of soda crackers, my bull whip! – *(Picks up whip from table.)* And five hundred dollars in cash. And, boy – *(Walking over to* **PURLIE***.)* I want it back!

LUTIEBELLE. Stealing ain't all that black and white.

MISSY. And we certainly wasn't the ones that started it!

GITLOW. Who stole me from Africa in the first place?

LUTIEBELLE. Who kept me in slavery from 1619 to 1863, working me to the bone without no social security?

PURLIE. And tonight – just because I went up that hill, and disembezzled my own inheritance that you stole from me –!

OL' CAP'N. *(Livid.)* I have had a belly full of your black African sass –!

> *(The door bursts open again; this time it is the* **SHERIFF** *who comes in with pistol drawn.)*

SHERIFF. All right, everybody, drop that gun!

PURLIE. Drop what gun?

OL' CAP'N. So there you are, you idiot – what kept you so long?

SHERIFF. Like you told us to do on the phone, suh, we was taking a good, long, slow snoop 'round and 'bout the commissary looking for clues! And dog-gone if one didn't, just a short while ago, stumble smack into our hands!

OL' CAP'N. What!

SHERIFF. We caught the culprit red-handed – bring in the prisoner, Dep!

DEPUTY. Glad to oblige you, Sheriff.

> *(Enter* **DEPUTY***, dragging* **CHARLIE***, who has his hands cuffed behind him; wears heavy leg shackles, and has a large white gag stuck into his mouth.)*

SHERIFF. Southern justice strikes again!

OL' CAP'N. Charlie! – oh, no!

IDELLA. Charlie, my baby!

OL' CAP'N. Release him, you idiots! Release him at once!

> *(Everybody pitches in to set* **CHARLIE** *free.)*

What have they done to you, my boy?

IDELLA. What have they done to you!

CHARLIE. *(Free from the gag.)* Hello, Paw – Idella – Purlie –

OL' CAP'N. I'll have your thick, stupid necks for this!

SHERIFF. It was you give the orders, suh!

OL' CAP'N. Not my son, you idiot!

DEPUTY. It was him broke into the commissary.

OL' CAP'N. What!

SHERIFF. It was him stole the five hundred dollars – he confessed!

OL' CAP'N. Steal? A Cotchipee? Suh, that is biologically impossible! *(To* **CHARLIE***.)* Charlie, my boy. Tell them the truth – tell them who stole the money. It was Purlie, wasn't it, boy?

CHARLIE. Well, as a matter of fact, Paw – it was mostly me that broke in and took the money, I'd say. In fact it WAS me!

OL' CAP'N. No!

CHARLIE. It was the only thing I could do to save your life, Paw.

OL' CAP'N. Save my life! Idella, he's delirious –!

CHARLIE. When Purlie come up that hill after you last night, I seen him, and lucky for you I did. The look he had on his face against you was not a Christian thing to behold! It was terrible! I had to get into that commissary, right then and there, open that safe, and pay him his inheritance – even then I had to beg him to spare your life!

OL' CAP'N. *(To* **PURLIE**.*)* You spare my life, boy? How dare you? *(To* **CHARLIE**.*)* Charlie, my son, I know you never recovered from the shock of losing your mother – almost before you were born. But don't worry – it was Purlie who stole that money and I'm going to prove it.

(Starts to take out gun. **GITLOW** *grabs gun.)*

Gitlow, my old friend, arrest this boy, Gitlow! As Deputy-For-The-Colored – I order you to arrest this boy for stealing!

GITLOW. *(With a brand new meaning.)* "Gone are the days –" *(Still twirls pistol safely out of* **OL' CAP'N**'*s reach.)*

PURLIE. "Stealin," is it? Well, I'm gonna really give you something to arrest me for. *(Snatches bull whip.)*

OL' CAP'N. Have a care, boy: I'm still a white man.

PURLIE. Congratulations! Twenty years ago, I told you this bull whip was gonna change hands one of these days!

MISSY. Purlie, wait –!

PURLIE. Stay out of my struggle for power!

MISSY. You can't do wrong just because it's right!

GITLOW. Never kick a man when he's down except in self-defense!

LUTIEBELLE. And no matter what you are, and always will be – the hero of Cotchipee Hill.

PURLIE. Am I?

LUTIEBELLE. Ten thousand queens!

PURLIE. I bow to the will of the Negro people. *(Throws whip away. Back to* **OL' CAP'N**.*)* But one thing, Ol' Cap'n, I am released of you – the entire Negro people is released of you! No more shouting hallelujah! every time you sneeze, nor jumping jackass every time you whistle "Dixie"! We gonna love you if you let us and laugh as we leave if you don't. We want our cut of the Constitution, and we want it now: and not with no teaspoon, white folks – throw it at us with a shovel!

OL' CAP'N. Charlie, my boy – my own, lily-white, Anglo-Saxon, semi-confederate son. I know you never recovered from the shock of losing your mother, almost before you were born. But don't worry: there is still time to take these insolent, messy cotton-picking ingrates down a peg – and prove by word and deed that God is still a white man. Tell 'em! Boy, tell 'em!

CHARLIE. Tell 'em what, Paw?

OL' CAP'N. Tell 'em what you and me have done together. Nobody here would believe me. Tell 'em how you went to Waycross, Saturday night, in my name –

CHARLIE. Yes, sir – I did.

OL' CAP'N. Tell 'em how you spoke to Ol' Man Pelham in my name –

CHARLIE. Yes, sir – I spoke to him.

OL' CAP'N. And paid him cash for that ol' barn they used to call Big Bethel!

CHARLIE. Yes, sir; that's what I did, all right.

OL' CAP'N. And to register the deed in the courthouse in my name –

CHARLIE. Yes, sir, that's exactly what you told me to do –

OL' CAP'N. Then – ain't but one thing left to do with that ramshackle dung-soaked monstrosity – that's burn the damn thing down. *(Laughs aloud in his triumph.)*

CHARLIE. But. Paw –

OL' CAP'N. First thing, though – let me see the deed: I wouldn't want to destroy nothing that didn't – legally – belong to me. *(Snatches deed from* **CHARLIE***'s hand. Begins to mumble as he reads it.)*

IDELLA. Twenty years of being more than a mother to you!

CHARLIE. Wait, Idella, wait. I did go to Waycross, like Paw said; I did buy the barn – excuse me, Purlie: the church – like he said; and I registered the deed at the courthouse like he told me – but not in Paw's name –

OL' CAP'N. *(Startled by something he sees on the deed.)* What's this?

CHARLIE. *(To* **IDELLA***.)* I registered the deed in the name of –

OL' CAP'N. *(Reading, incredulous.)* "Purlie Victorious Judson –" No!

IDELLA. PURLIE VICTORIOUS Judson?

OL' CAP'N. *(Choking on the words.)* Purlie Victorious Judsssss–aaaarrrrgggghhhhh! *(The horror of it strikes him absolutely still.)*

CHARLIE. *(Taking the deed from* **OL' CAP'N***'s limp hand.)* It was the only thing I could do to save your life. *(Offering deed to* **PURLIE***.)* Well, Purlie, here it is.

PURLIE. *(Counting out the five hundred dollars.)* You did a good job, Charlie – I'm much obliged!

CHARLIE. *(Refuses money; still holds out deed to **PURLIE**.)* Thank you, Purlie, but –

PURLIE. Big Bethel is my Bethel, Charlie: it's my responsibility. Go on, take it.

CHARLIE. No, no! I couldn't take your money, Purlie –

IDELLA. Don't be a fool, boy – business is business. *(She takes the deed from **CHARLIE** and gives it to **PURLIE**, while at the same time taking the money from **PURLIE**.)*

CHARLIE. Idella – I can't do that!

IDELLA. I can! I'll keep it for you.

CHARLIE. Well – all right. But only, if – if –

IDELLA. Only if what?

CHARLIE. *(To **PURLIE**.)* Would you let me be a member of your church?

MISSY. You?

GITLOW. Li'l Charlie Cotchipee!

LUTIEBELLE. A member of Big Bethel?

CHARLIE. May I? That is – that is, if you don't mind – as soon as you get it started?

PURLIE. Man, we're already started: the doors of Big Bethel, Church of the New Freedom for all Mankind, are hereby declared "Open for business"!

GITLOW. Brother Pastor, I move we accept Brother Charlie Cotchipee as our first candidate for membership to Big Bethel on a integrated basis –

MISSY. I second that motion!

PURLIE. You have heard the motion. Are you ready for the question?

ALL (EXCEPT OL' CAP'N). Question!

PURLIE. Those in favor will signify by saying "Aye."

> *(Everybody, except* **OL' CAP'N**, *crowds around* **CHARLIE**, *saying "Aye" over and over, in such a crescendo of welcome that* **PURLIE** *has to ride over the noise.)*

Those opposed?

> *(Looks at* **OL' CAP'N**, *who is still standing, as if frozen, as we last saw him. He does not answer.)*

Those opposed will signify by saying –

> *(He stops... all eyes focus on* **OL' CAP'N** *now, still standing in quiet, frozen-like immobility. There is a moment of silence, an unspoken suspicion in everybody's face. Finally,* **GITLOW** *goes over and touches* **OL' CAP'N**, *still standing rigid. Still he does not move.* **GITLOW** *feels his pulse, listens to his heart, and lifts up his eyelids. Nothing.)*

GITLOW. The first man I ever seen in all this world to drop dead standing up!

> *(Blackout.)*

Epilogue

(Time: Immediately following.)

(Scene: We are at Big Bethel at funeral services for Ol' Cap'n.)

(At Rise: We cannot see the coffin. We hear the ringing of the church bell as we come out of the blackout. **PURLIE** *is in the pulpit.)*

PURLIE. And toll the bell, Big Bethel, toll the bell! Dearly beloved, recently bereaved, and friends, we welcome you to Big Bethel, Church of the New Freedom: part Baptist; part Methodist; part Catholic – with the merriness of Christmas and the happiness of Hanukkah; and to the first integrated funeral in the sovereign, segregated state of Georgia. Let there be no merriments in these buryments! Though you are dead, Ol' Cap'n, and in hell, I suspect – as post-mortal guest of honor, at our expense: it is not too late to repent. We still need togetherness; we still need each otherness – with faith in the futureness of our cause. Let us, therefore, stifle the rifle of conflict, shatter the scatter of discord, smuggle the struggle, tickle the pickle, and grapple the apple of peace!

GITLOW. This funeral has been brought to you as a public service.

PURLIE. Take up his bones. For he who was my skin's enemy, was brave enough to die standing for what he believed... And it is the wish of his family – and his friends – that he be buried likewise –

(The **PALLBEARERS** *enter, carrying Ol' Cap'n's ornate coffin just as he would have wished: standing up! It is draped in a Confederate flag; and his hat, his bull whip, and his pistol, have been fastened to the lid in appropriate places.)*

PURLIE. Gently, gently. Put kindness in your fingers. He was a man – despite his own example. Take up his bones.

*(The **PALLBEARERS** slowly carry the upright coffin across the stage.)*

Tonight, my friends – I find, in being black, a thing of beauty: a joy; a strength; a secret cup of gladness; a native land in neither time nor place – a native land in every Negro face! Be loyal to yourselves: your skin; your hair; your lips, your southern speech, your laughing kindness – are Negro kingdoms, vast as any other! Accept in full the sweetness of your blackness – not wishing to be red, nor white, nor yellow: nor any other race, or face, but this. Farewell, my deep and Africanic brothers, be brave, keep freedom in the family, do what you can for the white folks, and write me in care of the post office. Now, may the Constitution of the United States go with you; the Declaration of Independence stand by you; the Bill of Rights protect you; and the State Commission Against Discrimination keep the eyes of the law upon you, henceforth, now and forever. Amen.

Curtain

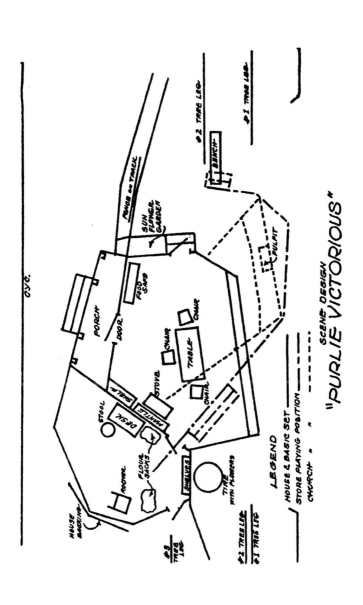

SCENE DESIGN
"PURLIE VICTORIOUS"